• *World Famous* •

# THEY LOST A FORTUNE

*. World Famous .*

# THEY LOST A FORTUNE

**Jacqueline Mroz**

**MAGPIE**
London

Magpie Books Ltd
11 Shepherd House
Shepherd Street
London W1Y 7LD

First published in the UK
by Magpie Books Ltd in 1992

Copyright Robinson Publishing © 1992

Illustrations © Popperfoto

ISBN 1 85487 156 0
ISBN 1 85813 120 0
10 9 8 7 6 5 4 3 2 1

Printed in Finland by
Werner Söderström Oy

*For Simon*

# Contents

# INTRODUCTION

Two of the most fascinating and constant features of wealth are its fragility and capriciousness. In 1991, billionaire media magnate Robert Maxwell was Britain's eighth richest man – within one year he became the world's first minus-billionaire. Thousands of pensioners were left with empty pockets after the publisher used their hard-earned savings to cover his losses. Many of the other minus-millionaires found in this book are entrepreneurs who made it big in the 1980s – that decade of greed, excess and unbelievably huge profits. The start of the 1990s proved to be a cold slap in the face for these fortune-hunters, with high interest rates, recession and collapsing property values draining their Swiss bank accounts.

But recession is just one way of losing big money. Swindlers like Ivan Boesky and Michael Milken became obsessed with making money, duping their victims for years, but were finally brought to justice by financial watchdogs. There are those like Donald "The Donald" Trump, Asil Nadir, and Australians Alan Bond and Robert Holmes à Court who made bad investments or faulty financial deals involving millions of dollars. High living is a tried and trusted way of frittering away a fortune, with practitioners like eccentric billionaire Howard Hughes who used Kleenex tissues at an alarming rate (he was obsessed with germs) and hotel king and queen Leona and Harry Helmsley who thought the "little people" should pay taxes. For some, things just didn't work out, like boxer Mike Tyson, train robber Ronald Biggs, and

Country and Wester singer Willie Nelson. And finally, there are those exiled aristocrats such as the Shah of Iran who believed he was "chosen" to lead his country by divine forces, and famous shoe consumers Ferdinand and Imelda Marcos who saw their luxurious lifestyles change dramatically when they were banished from their homes.

Still, one can always be assured that people will find new ways of making money, and even more ways of losing it.

# · chapter one ·

# SWINDLERS

*D*id their greediness or egomania get the better of them? There is one fundamental objective for a swindler and that is to make as much money as possible without worrying how, and who, they go about getting it from. They are very confident people, who do not tolerate being told what, and what not, to do – and that is usually their downfall.

## John De Lorean

John De Lorean started his career with seemingly everything going for him. He was General Motors's "Golden Haired Boy" who could do no wrong, and swiftly moved up the corporate ladder into the GM executive suite. He later became famous for his "winged" De Lorean sports car and for his involvement with a string of beautiful women. Little did anyone know that he was set on a course for disaster.

Born in Detroit, "the Motor City", in 1925, the son of a Ford employee, he had cars in his blood. His family was poor – De Lorean once told how he wore the same suit from the time he was twelve until he left college. After graduating from university he decided to try his hand at selling advertising space for the Yellow Pages. The only problem was that the Michigan Bell telephone company published the other Yellow Pages (the original version) and attempted to have De Lorean tried for fraud. He managed to extract himself from his predicament by paying back all of the businesses he had taken money from.

After this experience, De Lorean decided to switch tacks and enroled at the Chrysler Institute as an engineering trainee. He did a stint working for the Packard Company for a few years and changed over to GM when they folded. He soon became the youngest general manager of the Pontiac Division, and was later tapped to take charge of the fast-growing Chevrolet Division. Under his management, Pontiac's image was changed from that of a maker of an old lady's car into a racy powerhouse bestseller. He introduced important engineering innovations, such as the overhead cam engine, the concealed windshield wiper, and the radio antenna embedded in the windshield. While De Lorean was head of Chevrolet, nearly 3.5 million cars were made a year – more than any other car company before them. The company went from a twenty-year downward trend to its most profitable years and De Lorean seemed to have the GM presidency in his hand.

By this time De Lorean, who was tall, elegant and hand-some, had become obsessed with his appearance and had undergone plastic surgery to make his chin square and rugged looking, as well as a nose job. He also changed other aspects of his life, including divorcing his wife of fifteen years. He started dating beautiful women such as Ursula Andress, Candice Bergen, and Nancy Sinatra, then married Kelly Harmon, the nineteen-year-old daughter of an American football hero. De Lorean later divorced her to marry well-known fashion model Cristina Ferrare, then twenty-three and known as the Max Factor girl.

He radiated immense power and energy to everyone he met and was admired within the automobile industry for his credibility. Auto News wrote when he left GM: "Now, more than ever before the industry needs the colour and style of a De Lorean." Others, however, said De Lorean had been in mental and moral decline since he took over Chevrolet and had been involved in some shady deals. At this time he also began investing heavily in things such as real estate, oil fields, and football teams. Before taking over Chevrolet, De Lorean was described as portly. But once the phone calls from Hollywood started coming in to this newly powerful man, he became a health freak and lost about 40lbs.

In 1973, De Lorean left General Motors. Rumours abounded that he was asked to leave for taking kickbacks from Chevrolet dealers. GM top management had also reportedly become concerned about both damaging leaks concerning information about new product designs, problems with dealers, and production schedules, and De Lorean's increasingly erratic behaviour. After hiring a private detective to track down the leaks, it was found that they were coming from De Lorean himself. When confronted with this information, the former Golden Boy threatened to go public with other embarrassing documents about the company and they finally settled on an agreement: De Lorean would leave GM with a settlement of a $1 million Cadillac dealership in Florida.

De Lorean then tried to make it in various businesses and failed – with many ending in litigation and questions about his business ethics. The first of these was a business De Lorean started with two of his brothers called Grand Prix Ltd, which franchised race tracks around the US with tiny racing cars. The venture ended with the company filing for bankruptcy in November 1975, and one of his brothers suing him. They were also charged with fraud by a man who was tricked into buying $100,000 of Grand Prix stock.

Next, De Lorean came up with the idea of manufacturing two-seat sportscars with the distinguishing feature of having doors that opened up instead of out, like wings. The car would have a slew of safety features. The idea was not an original one, however. The year before a man from Phila-delphia named Malcolm Bricklin had attempted to design, manufacture and sell a similar car, but failed when it was found that the cars were riddled with problems.

In 1975 the De Lorean Sports Car Partnership was created, with a projection of selling thirty-five cars at $100,000 each. After having difficulties in finding a location to set up his plant, the British government of James Callaghan stepped in and offered the use of Belfast as a site in return for various subsidies. They never investigated his background nor questioned his reasons for leaving his job with GM that had paid him $700,000 a year. The deal was expected to bring sorely needed business to the struggling Irish city, which was one of the poorest areas in Europe. De Lorean cut a deal with the British which gave him $97 million, one-third of which was a grant, with a promise of $20 million more if employment goals were reached. The British government was never to see that money again. In 1980 De Lorean employed 1,000 people and the company was rapidly growing. But soon debts began to pile up and cars were slow to come off the assembly line. The company was in trouble. De Lorean began looking for more investors and new bank loans. Some company funds were allegedly used to finance a personal land deal in California that he was negotiating, and $8.9 million was used to refinance his purchase of a ski-slope snow grooming equipment business in Logan, Utah. He then turned to the British government again, asking for more funds, but was turned down and an audit of the company's books was ordered. De Lorean scrambled to find the money to cover his debts and avoid bankruptcy, and was nearly successful. But he was duped, because the drug deal which was going to save De Lorean's company was a set-up by the US Federal Bureau of Investigation. They convinced him that if he helped them with the deal to import drugs into America, he would receive $10 million working capital instantly and another $50 million on the way. James Hoffman, an old friend of De Lorean's who had turned informer for the DEA set up the deal, which the automobile manufacturer saw as his only hope of rescuing the "dream car". Meanwhile, the FBI agent who posed as the "Mr Big" who would finance the deal for half of the De Lorean motor company, and the banker who would launder the money were recording every incriminating word spoken by De Lorean – fifty-eight telephone conversations in all were taped. On 19 October 1982, FBI and Drug Enforcement Agency agents arrested him for allegedly selling $16 million worth of cocaine. And they had it on videotape.

De Lorean's defence lawyer, Howard Weitzman, had successfully defended other seemingly hopeless cases: alleged Mafia capos and brutal killers and even got a member of the Manson family off a murder charge – the only one out of the group to go free. The attorney managed to delay the case for seventeen months, then exploited his client's glamour to build public sympathy for him. He eventually convinced the jury that he had been entrapped: the law enforcers had gone beyond permissible measures to seize a suspect and had set up the conspiracy which snared De Lorean. Weitzman also used De Lorean's high-profile wife, Cristina Ferrare, by advising her how to dress and act in the courtroom and sending her to appear on television talk shows and defend her husband. During the trial, Ferrare, who was a born-again Christian, convinced De Lorean to convert to Christianity. Just when the jury seemed ready to give a verdict, he was baptised in his ornamental swimming pool of his 400-acre estate in Bedminster, New Jersey, with Cristina at his side wearing a long white gown. He wore a drip-dry leisure suit.

De Lorean managed to evade jail on a technicality and walked away a free, though considerably poorer, man. He left behind him a pile of debts amounting to more than $250 million, as well as $17.5 million that was never accounted for. The British government was out £84 million, 2,600 De Lorean factory workers were out of a job, and the Northern Ireland economy – already in a slump – was dealt another blow. In addition to the failure of his empire, his third wife left him.

# Horatio Bottomley

Horatio Bottomley was born with the gift of gab, and could charm almost anyone into giving him their money. He rose to become a well-known politician and an expert conman. Born in the East End of London in 1860, he knew early on that he wanted fame, women and a brilliant political career. But making money, and lots of it, was his dream. Bottomley helped start the *Financial Times* and the patriotic magazine *John Bull*, and was later elected to represent Hackney South – a London constituency – as a Member of Parliament. He lived the life of a local squire with his wife in Upper Dicker near Sussex, and kept a series of mistresses all over England.

Bottomley began working as a clerk for a solicitor, then went to work as a shorthand writer at the Law Courts in London. Next, he started a publishing company along with some friends; bought some properties and a printing works in Devon for £200,000 from a friend. He then sold them to the publishing company for £325,000. Bottomley's colleagues charged him with fraud when they found out that most of the properties weren't worth anything – something he already knew. The conman decided to defend himself during his trial, and won, impressing the judge so much by his technique that he was told to think about becoming a lawyer. From one swindle to another: Bottomley's next target was the Australian gold boom. He eventually made a small bundle of money by promoting the gold mines, though his firms habitually failed and he was regularly served with bankruptcy writs. Yet, he never had any trouble finding people to invest in his ventures.

Bottomley's scheme was to start a company and announce high dividends, then he and his co-horts would sell the shares once their price increased. When the business started to fail, he would create another one and use the new shareholders' money to buy up the old company. In 1912, the conman was forced to resign from Parliament when a bankruptcy case he was involved in was made public. During the war he used his magazine to support Britain's efforts and recruit soldiers. His patience paid off and he was re-elected as an MP for his constituency in 1918. Bottomley operated his last swindle the next year, when he began selling government-issued Victory Bonds through a club to working-class people who couldn't afford the full price of £5. Investors could spend whatever they wanted, with the club picking up the rest of the tab for them. Bottomley, however, was skimming money off the top, and by the time he was discovered he had taken £150,000 of the investors' cash. Within the six months the scheme ran, he had spent most of the money already on paying off debts, horse-racing, and buying and exhibiting a German submarine. He was prosecuted in 1922 for fraudulent conversion of funds and sentenced to seven years in prison. The former millionaire died penniless in 1933.

# Robert Maxwell

"Captain" Bob Maxwell lived much as he died – mysteriously and surrounded by publicity. The billionaire press lord's naked body was found floating in the ocean off the Canary Islands, six hours after the crew of his yacht, the

Lady Ghislaine, had reported him missing. Circumstances surrounding his death, or the cause of it, are still unknown and may never be discovered, but one thing is known: Maxwell, sixty-eight, was deeply in debt when he died.

Although he was thought to have a fortune of £1.2 billion, making him Britain's eighth richest man when he died, Maxwell in fact left behind a legacy of unpaid bills and crumbling businesses. It was later revealed that the publisher had been making inter-company loans; using the money from his companies' pension funds to cover losses in other companies. The collapse of his empire has left many employees without jobs and hundreds without pensions. Many shareholders have been left with worthless investments. A week after Maxwell's death it emerged that his companies owed banks £758 million, and the value of shares in the businesses had collapsed. Investigators discovered that a total of £297 million was missing, owed to Maxwell Communications and Mirror Group Newspapers, and finally realized the extent to which Maxwell had plundered his companies. After a full investigation it was revealed that total liabilities for the company had risen to £1.8 billion (assets were worth about £800 million), and that Maxwell had taken £245 million from MCC, and £97 million from MGN. Total losses in pensions were £429 million, with bank debts at about £1 billion. Months after his death, investigators were still examining the Maxwell papers to figure out just how much the former press baron had lost.

Maxwell's rags-to-riches story began in Solotvino, Czechoslovakia, where he was born Ludvik Hoch in 1923 to a Hasidic Jewish family of impoverished labourers. As a child Maxwell often went hungry, and only had three years of formal education. He apparently joined the Czech resistance movement against the Nazis when he was fifteen, and later took to selling trinkets to earn a living. He lost most of his family in the Holocaust. As a youth he fled to France where he fought in the French resistance movement and met his French wife Elisabeth Meynard, before he escaped to England.

In England he joined the British Army, became a captain and was later awarded the Military Cross for heroism for fighting in Normandy. A few years later, in 1949, he borrowed money from his in-laws and founded Pergamon Press – a company that imported and distributed German scientific journals in Britain. The business made him a millionaire.

In later years he boasted that he launched Pergamon with £13,000 and sold it for £446 million. He later became a world leader in the field of scientific journals and set himself the goal of becoming the world's largest printer.

During this time he and his wife had nine children, among them Kevin and Ian who were just three years apart in age and later came to help their father run his empire. The success of Pergamon enabled Maxwell to win a seat in the House of Commons as a Labour MP in 1964. Four years later he left office after failing to become a cabinet minister due to financial finagling, but was a committed life-long Labour party member. He had been courted by the Conservatives – including ex-Prime Minister Margaret Thatcher – to join their party, but had turned them down. During the 1987 election campaign, he refused to publish a three-page advertisement for the then desperate Tories, making a slew of enemies within the Conservative party.

In 1980, Maxwell once again proved his worth as a businessman, buying the heavily indebted British Printing Corporation and turning it into a successful operation. Maxwell, who was quickly bored, then decided to move into newspapers and book publishing. It took him a while to acquire the newspapers he wanted to buy, but in 1984 he purchased the racy London tabloid, the *Daily Mirror*, and entered into a media war with Australian media baron Rupert Murdoch who owned *The Sun* tabloid. Under Maxwell's leadership, the circulation of the *Daily Mirror* increased from 200,000 to 3.6 million. He also bought a stake in MTV Europe. The *Daily Mirror*'s success, however, didn't extend to all his other holdings. The *London Daily News*, launched in 1987, lasted only five months. In May 1990 Maxwell launched *The European*, a daily European newspaper, after failed attempts to buy the *National Enquirer*, America's biggest selling tabloid, as well as three other American tabloids.

Maxwell loved America and was anxious to move into the US market. He ended up paying huge sums for media properties there in the late 1980s – he paid $2.6 billion for Macmillan Inc. publishers in 1988 – and his expansion into the United States left him heavily leveraged. In February 1991, however, Maxwell indulged himself once more and began making tenuous inquiries into the purchase the strike-ridden New York *Daily News*. In the years before, Maxwell had regularly phoned the News's publisher to ask if the paper was for sale. Until then he hadn't had a chance. When the deal finally went through, with the unions making important concessions, the *Daily News*'s headline read "Cap'n Bob bites the Big Apple". Many considered Maxwell a hero at the time – he had saved the *Daily News* from the grave.

Maxwell was legendary for being incredibly hard working – he normally worked 14-16 hour days – and for being incredibly difficult to work for. He liked to rule his employees by fear and demanded that they work as hard as he did. The media magnate would often fire employees at will. He once even fired his son, Ian Maxwell, for failing to meet his plane at Orly airport in Paris. When his helicopter landed at the Daily Mirror building in central London, staff would run through the building sounding the warning, saying: "The Ego Has Landed."

When Russian troops invaded Lithuania in 1990, Maxwell's newly appointed *Daily Mirror* editor Roy Greenslade (a former senior editor at the *Sunday Times*) had his newspaper cover the event. Maxwell rang Greenslade to tell him to cease reporting negatively about the actions taken by Gorbachev, whom he considered a good friend. Greenslade understandably objected to Maxwell's interference, pointing out that "news is news". Maxwell responded by saying that Gorbachev would not do anything without consulting him first. Soon after Greenslade was sacked.

Maxwell considered himself a media magnate and enjoyed being compared to publishing giant William Randolph Hearst (*see* page 63). He liked to have his ego stroked and would often take would-be calls from the White House while visitors to his office (especially bankers) waited to speak to him. Cap'n Bob liked to believe that he was a powerful and influential world figure and international statesman, and enjoyed the welcomes he received at foreign airports, and the waiving of passport formalities.

He did, however, hold strong ties to the communist leaders, including East Germany's Erick Honecker. He met with him shortly before the Berlin Wall came down, and was later criticized for being a fair-weather friend to the leader. Before Honecker was removed from office, Maxwell described him as having been a reformer all his life.

"I have played a major part in the changes that have taken place in many of these countries, as is best evidenced by the fact that I'm playing a leading part with the new people.

Why? Because I have always been a professed, strong anti-Communist," said Maxwell in an interview. He did admit, however, that he had made mistakes in his associations with East European leaders, (in the past he lauded leaders such as Romanian despot Nikolae Ceausescu) but that his mistakes were not in befriending them but in not saying publicly how critical he was of them.

Maxwell also expanded his business interests into Eastern Europe and invested heavily in newspapers there. He travelled extensively and spent at least nine days a month in New York. A committed Zionist, he oversaw an airlift of ailing Soviet Jewish children from the Chernobyl area to Israel in 1990 and later visited them there by helicopter.

All the flying and overwork, along with his being about 90lbs overweight, led to health problems. Although Maxwell suffered from chronic colds made worse by the partial removal of a lung thirty years ago, he never slowed his pace. Even with all the pressures he was feeling from his business problems, Captain Bob would never have let it show. His strategy was to never panic.

We will never know, however, if that is what Maxwell did on the night of 5 November 1991 when his body was found floating in the Atlantic Ocean. Did the mountain of debt he had built up finally cause him to panic? Or was it an accident? Or perhaps murder . . .

According to investigators, Maxwell's behaviour shortly before his demise that night was out of character and strangely indecisive. He unexpectedly decided to take a trip on his yacht to help get over a cold, and did not bring any staff or guests aboard which was unusual for him.

The Lady Ghislaine was a colossal yacht Maxwell owned and operated and often used to entertain and impress his visitors. It had a main stateroom and four decks, and the crew consisted of thirteen and two chefs. The boat could be chartered for about £100,000 per week. Before boarding, guests were asked to take their shoes off.

He boarded the yacht in Gibraltar and planned to take a cruise over the next week to help recover from a cold. He was seen by a crew member on deck at about 4:25 a.m. – about half an hour before the time of death. Maxwell complained that he was warm and the air conditioning fans were switched on. About twenty minutes later he called the bridge and asked that the fans be turned off. He was never heard from again. The next morning, after a phone call from New York for him, Maxwell was found to be missing. That afternoon, after the alarm was sounded and rescue crews were notified, Maxwell's naked body was spotted floating in waters off the Canary Islands.

Maxwell's widow and eldest son, Philip, arrived to identify the remains, which were then flown to Jerusalem on a chartered jet for burial. The oversized casket containing Maxwell's 286lb body, however, did not fit onto Maxwell's private jet and a larger plane had to be ordered.

Insurance investigators who hold the £20 million life policy on the publisher are still trying to determine exactly how Maxwell died. But an official report issued in February 1992 indicates that they consider suicide the most credible answer. They have ruled out a heart attack, though not completely, because they say if this had occurred he would have been more likely to have fallen down on deck and are quite certain he could not have rolled from the deck into the sea. Loss adjustors have also excluded the possibility of murder, because, they say, there is simply no evidence to suggest it. One of the reasons they say suicide was the cause of his death is that he was unusually "complimentary and almost amicable towards the crew". The reports suggests that it was conceivable that he had reached the conclusion that the collapse of the empire was inevitable. "We wonder whether Robert Maxwell's decision to spend those last days on the Lady Ghislaine, his request that his jet rendezvous with the yacht at sea and his unusually pleasant manner the majority of the time, were brought about by Robert Maxwell's realization that the end of his business career and his flamboyant lifestyle was rapidly drawing to a close," the report says.

Dr Iain West, a noted British pathologist who conducted a second post-mortem examination on the body of Robert Maxwell before it was interred in Israel, says his findings suggest that the cause of death was probably drowning.

In the year before he died, Maxwell began selling off his assets in an effort to shrink his debt. When he died his companies were about $4 billion in the red. A few days after he died the sale of Berlitz International, a language training organization, was finalized. The Japanese publishers Fukutake purchased the company for $265 million. Still, this was not enough to save Maxwell Communications Corporation and his other companies from an uncertain future. After

Maxwell's death, MCC, which included Macmillan Publishing, Collier's Encyclopedia and Official Airline Guides, was in debt for $2.5 billion. In the 1991 financial year its revenues had been $2 billion. Mirror Group Newspapers, including the *Daily Mirror* and four other British newspapers, was in hock for $583 million with yearly revenues of $792 million. And Robert Maxwell Group Ltd, which comprised the New York *Daily News*, *The European* and the Oxford United Football Club was $1.3 billion in debt with revenues unknown. With all of his holdings, Maxwell was not producing enough money to pay off his loans; he was paying $290 million in interest on the $2.6 billion he had borrowed.

Maxwell liked to describe himself as being not just a hero, but a cult figure. His main strength was his extraordinary courage but his major fault was his intimidation of the weak; there were few who mourned his passing, except those to whom he owed money.

# Ivan Boesky

In the fall of 1986 the United States Securities and Exchange Commission moved in on the man who was once called the greediest man on earth – Ivan Boesky. His name was to come to represent the end of the Eighties' greed and a finish to the reign of those Wall Street financiers who made millions of dollars for themselves and their clients during this golden era.

Boesky, fifty-five, was Wall Street's most flamboyant personality and most feared arbitrageur before his arrest for using inside information to buy and sell shares. He was sent to jail for three years and fined $100 million in return for naming those involved in his deals and identifying specific trades as part of a plea-bargain agreement with federal prosecutors. Before his fall, Boesky claimed he was earning $1,700 an hour, though most of the money he was playing with was not his. He was nicknamed "Piggy" for his singlemindedness and is believed to have borrowed more than $2 billion to finance his deals.

By nature a secretive man, Boesky was part of the mysterious world of Wall Street arbitrage, where they are known as "arbs". These financial gamblers set themselves apart from the establishment by taking advantage of its inefficiencies – buying and selling stocks of companies involved in real or rumoured take-overs. Huge profit eventually brought these people respectability, something Boesky craved.

But perhaps even more than respect, Boesky craved money – lots of it. His famous speech where he espoused that "greed is good", was used by filmmaker Oliver Stone in his film "Wall Street", and the main character – a powerful Wall Street tycoon who is investigated by government authorities and jailed for illegal trading – is loosely based on Boesky.

For Boesky, the perfect aphrodisiac was "climbing to the top of a Jacob's ladder of silver dollars", and possessions and credentials were his nectar. He commuted by limousine to Wall Street from his luxurious estate in Westchester County and flew around the world in a personal, leased jet.

No one knows exactly how much money he has (or had), but after paying a fine $100 million to the Federal Government, he reportedly was still left with a few hundred

Even Victorian England had its version of swindlers like today's Robert Maxwell. In the late 1800s, Jabez Balfour, a respected man who was a Justice of the Peace, a Member of Parliament, and a mayor of a London suburb, devised the snowballing technique whereby one company finances another. When discovered, Balfour was about to accept an important government post and had to leave the country – fleeing to South America – to avoid prosecution. His crime was persuading people to invest cash in phoney businesses. Eventually, his money-making schemes spun out of control and one of his companies went bust in 1892, owing £8 million. But by the time the government realized what Balfour had been doing for the past twenty years, this swindler was already on his way to South America to escape. Three years later while living in Salta, Chile, he was recognized by a tourist who immediately reported his presence to the British Consul. Balfour was eventually extradited to England where he stood trial at the Old Bailey for swindling his investors out of millions. He was sentenced to fourteen years of prison and died of a heart attack shortly after he served his time.

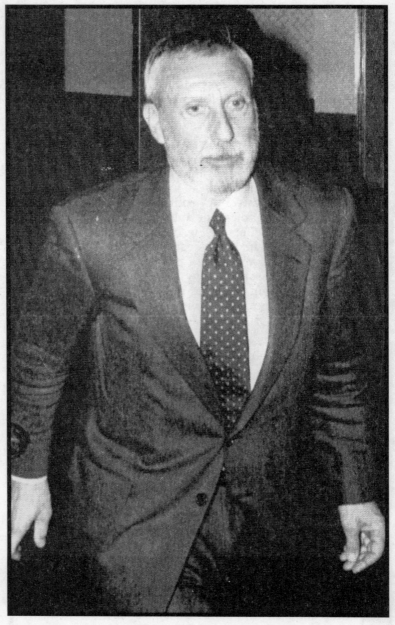

Ivan Boesky, pictured after a two year prison sentence.

million dollars. Shortly before his arrest and the public announcement of his co-operation agreement with the Feds, Boesky was allowed, as part of the deal, to sell off his arbitrage positions – something other arbs complained about because he had thus been allowed to insider-trade ahead of the announcement of having insider-traded.

Boesky also sold his assets to his wife days before his agreement with the government was made public. They included four per cent of the Beverly Hills Hotel and an interest in an Oklahoma television station. He also borrowed several million dollars from his wife. Part of Boesky's deal was that his wife and children would not be penalized by the government.

Since his trial and imprisonment, the disgraced Wall Street tycoon and his wife have split up and he is now suing his wife for more than $20,000 a week alimony – which he says he needs and deserves. This follows recent moves by his wife Seema to end their thirty-year marriage. Although Boesky reportedly made more than a billion dollars in his deals while insider-trading, he claims he has been virtually wiped out. The couple still own a Park Avenue penthouse in Manhattan, however, as well as a seventeen-room mansion set in seventy-five acres in New York state, an apartment in Paris and a house on the Cote d'Azur.

"I should not be forced to incur further debt while Seema re-decorates the marital estate and her penthouse apartment and has personal expenses of $50,000 a month," he said. Boesky was reportedly so embarrassed by his civil suit that it is listed as Anonymous I v Anonymous II in court documents. Keeping up appearances has always been important to this financial wizard who held meetings at New York's Harvard Club, though he never attended the university. He was considered an "outsider" when he first arrived on Wall Street in 1966 and joined New York securities analysts L. F. Rothschild, but later found his niche in arbitrage.

Boesky was born to Russian immigrants in Detroit, Michigan in 1937, and attended the University of Michigan, though he did not graduate. He then managed to obtain a degree from the Detroit College of Law which did not require an undergraduate degree to enter. During this time he met and married Seema Silberstein, the daughter of a Detroit real estate magnate who owned the Beverly Hills Hotel.

In 1975, he laid the first cornerstone of his empire when

he borrowed $700,000 from his wife's mother and founded
Boesky & Co., the first partnership devoted solely to securities arbitrage. He later changed the name to the Ivan F.
Boesky Corporation which became one of the largest arbitrage
firms on Wall Street, and began undertaking incredible coups;
he made millions on the Standard Oil of California take-over
and on the Eagle Star take-over by BAT. He also did well on
the outcome of the two-way Distillers battle that resulted with
Guinness chairman Ernest Saunders (*see* page 48) in jail.

But his incredible successes did not come about from
any inner investment wisdom – Boesky was paying Drexel
Burnham Lambert Inc managing director Dennis Levine
for inside information relating to tender offers, mergers
and extraordinary corporate transactions. Boesky apparently knew this information was confidential and had been
obtained through misappropriation. He was paying Levine
five per cent of the profits he made in dealings in securities
where Levine had provided confidential information. This
was later changed to an agreement where Boesky paid Levine
one per cent of all net profits he made on securities in which
he already controlled holdings, about which Levine supplied
confidential information.

One of the most prominent deals which Boesky made a
fortune from based on inside information, was the merger
between Nabisco Brands and R. J. Reynolds. Once Levine
obtained the information about the possible merger, he called
Boesky with the news. Boesky then instructed associate companies to buy 337,000 shares in Nabisco. The next day Nabisco
announced that exploratory merger talks with Reynolds had
begun, and Boesky and his companies immediately sold off
all their Nabisco shares for a profit of $4 million.

Although the SEC estimates that Boesky turned a profit of
at least $50 million through deals like this one, others estimate
he actually pulled in close to $1 billion. Much of this money
was used by Boesky to gain him the place in society he felt
he deserved.

He began donating money to Harvard, endowed a library
at the Jewish Theological Seminary and taught classes at
New York University and Brandeis University. He also
supported New York's Shakespeare Theatre and the Metropolitan Museum of Art. All this was done to gain acceptance
and respectability, but Boesky never really became a part of
the establishment.

According to a former associate of this most famous of arbs, Boesky's goal was to build one of the richest families in America. His personal philosophy is evident in a T-shirt he owns which reads "He who owns the most when he dies wins."

# Michael Milken

The man who aided Ivan Boesky (*see* page 14) in his deals and had the most to gain from them was junk bond king Michael Milken, who has the distinction of paying the highest individual criminal fine in history – $600 million.

When Milken, the man who was responsible for the creation and success of junk bonds, was sentenced by US District Judge Kimba Wood to ten years in prison for his crimes, he wept openly. This was the harshest sentence given out in the financial scandals that rocked Wall Street in the Eighties. Milken, forty-four-years-old when he was convicted in November 1990, was the man who ran what was referred to as the California crime centre – Drexel Burnham Lambert's Beverly Hills-based high-yield bond department. At the time, US prosecutors said this was a virtual command centre for a highly sophisticated financial crime ring led by Boesky and Milken.

"What I did violated not just the law but all my principles and values and I will regret it for the rest of my life. I am truly sorry," said Milken during his trial. He admitted to six fraud and conspiracy charges, but hoped to get off with just community service because of his record of philanthropic activities. The judge in his case, however, said that the junk bond financier had showed a pattern of skirting the law and cutting legal corners, and insisted that a prison sentence was one of the most powerful deterrents to the financial community.

Milken was sentenced to prison and three years' probation, shortly after his co-conspirator, Boesky, was released upon serving his three-year sentence. The pair enjoyed a lucrative partnership by manipulating markets and stocks and then capitalizing on them. Boesky would instruct his employees to take trading directions from the "Coast", presenting Milken with the opportunity to unlawfully influence and manipulate the equity securities markets. But it was Boesky who implicated him and sent the Wall Street financier to Pleasanton Federal Prison in California in the end.

Michael Milken reigned over the junk bond markets in the 1980s and his name soon became synonymous with financial excess. He was regarded by his supporters and many others as a financial wizard who broke the laws as a way of gaining competitive advantage in the $200 billion market he invented and dominated. Some still consider Milken, who earned an unbelievable $1.1 billion between 1983 and 1987, and made $550 million in salary and bonus in one year alone, to be a financial genius, economic visionary and generous philanthropist. In the late 1980s his family fortune was estimated to be worth $1.6 billion.

But others condemn him for defrauding investors and leaving behind a damaging legacy of huge junk bond debts which led to a number of savings and loan banks in the US to collapse. Despite paying a total of $1.1 billion to settle criminal and civil charges brought by government regulators and his former employers – Drexel Burnham Lambert – Milken is still a millionaire many times over.

# chapter two

# BAD INVESTMENTS OR FINANCIAL DEALS

*H*ow *do you make millions only to lose it all? Investment does does not always ensure accumulating a lot of money, it also means you can lose it, sometimes overnight, just as easily.*

## Donald Trump

His name is synonymous with 1980s greed, glitz and gambling. But 1990 didn't have such great things in store for New York's real estate magnate Donald Trump, whose businesses began crumbling with the collapse of junk bonds. Worth at one time more than $3 billion, Trump's assets are now estimated to be valued at minus $1.4 billion, (he says those figures are wrong, and that he is actually worth $1.5 billion). Trump was once regarded as a master of making megadollar deals – some said everything he touched turned to gold. Now, however, he is seen as a washed-up real estate mogul who nearly lost everything, as well as the man who left Ivana ("Ivana Divorce") Trump for a younger woman. He is not by any means a has-been, but he is definitely not the powerful tycoon he used to be.

Real estate seems to have been in the stars for Trump, the son of real estate developer Fred C. Trump. As a young boy he would glue toy blocks together into one giant skyscraper; when he was older he would spend his summers working at his father's construction sites, along with his brothers. This is where he developed his love for real estate: "I learned a lot about real estate just through osmosis from my father. But what really made it appeal to me as a career was the creativity involved," said Trump. At the age of thirty-six, he was a resounding success and had already accomplished in real estate nearly everything he had set out to do. No other New York City real estate developer has attracted so much public attention at such as early age. Trump is a controversial figure and his buildings are some of the most luxurious, ostentatious and expensive in New York City.

The building which sealed his reputation for putting his name to glitzy, grandiose projects is the Trump Tower, which was built at a cost estimated at $200 million and opened for occupancy in 1982. Located next door to Tiffany's on Fifth Avenue, it is the most expensive reinforced structure in New York City. Its residents include celebrities such as Johnny Carson, David Merrick and Sophia Loren. The peach-marble atrium contains an eighty-foot waterfall as well as restaurants and shops such as Charles Jourdan, whose first year's rent was reportedly $1 million. "I'll be thirty-six years old when Trump Tower opens, and I'll have done everything I can do, and sometimes I think, maybe it was a mistake to have raced through it all so fast," said Trump. Top-of-the-line two-bedroom flats in Trump Tower can be bought for about $2.25 million.

Trump was born in 1946 in the wealthy Jamaica Estates section of Queens, New York City to Fred and Mary Trump. He has two sisters and two brothers – the eldest of which died several years ago. His father was so young when he started out in the real estate business in 1923 that he had to ask for his mother's signature for leases. The Trump family was competitive and knew how to make a buck, according to Fred, Snr. As a youth, Donald was sent to the New York Military Academy, where he was elected captain of a student regiment as well as of the baseball team. He was considered a real leader and a better than average baseball player. His former baseball coach said he was good enough that the White Sox sent out a scout to watch him play. While attending the University of Pennsylvania Wharton School of Finance, Trump told fellow classmates that he wanted to change the

Manhattan skyline. He was bored there because most of his real estate classes were teaching how to build single family houses rather than how to develop skyscrapers. While still at university, Trump helped his father negotiate real estate deals. When he finished school, he knew what he wanted to do next – develop real estate. He joined his father at the Trump Organization and helped him build middle-income apartment houses in Queens, Brooklyn and Staten Island. Trump was given free reign by his father, who has said of him: "He has great vision, and everything he touches seems to turn to gold."

In 1973, Trump, who looked to 1950s real estate giant William Zeckendorf as his inspiration, decided to begin developing property in New York City. One of the first achievements which moved him into the world of real estate high rollers was convincing the city to build a multi-million dollar convention centre on property he owned – this when the city was desperately strapped for cash. Although he received a commission of $500,000, with $80,000 in expenses for the sale of the property, he said he would have accepted less if the city fathers had agreed to name the centre after his father.

Peter Solomon, former deputy mayor for economic development for NYC at the time said Trump impressed him: "What really got me was his bravado. I think it was fantastic. It was unbelievable. He almost got us to name the convention centre after his father in return for something he never really had to give away. I guess he just thought we would never read the fine print or, by the time we did, the deal to name the building after his father would have been set."

Another stepping stone for Trump into the world of high-profile developers was his purchase and development of the Commodore Hotel, which he turned into the classy Grand Hyatt Hotel. His father disapproved of him buying the building, which had been losing $1.5 million a year and had not paid any city taxes for several years, but Trump persisted. He negotiated a forty-year tax abatement with the city, the first granted to a commercial property. Many city officials grumbled that the deal was too lucrative for Trump – some hotel experts valued the tax break at about $45 million – and said the city could have made a better deal. But Trump made his deal at the right time, and in the right place. The hotel was located on East 42nd Street before it became a desirable place to live and work. This was one of Trump's maxims: "location, location, location". Another aspect of his personal philosophy was influenced by his family's minister, the Reverend Norman Vincent Peale. From him, Trump learned the power of positive thinking, and that the mind can overcome any obstacle: "I never think of the negative," he has said.

"Negotiation is an art, and I have a gift for it," Trump once said. He considers building an art form and has been described as being such a formidable salesman that he could sell sand to the Arabs and refrigerators to the Eskimos. He has been called a megalomaniac, and a visionary. His latest book, *Surviving at the Top*, was ironically released just as his empire began crumbling. He has been headline news for several years and once took out a full page newspaper advertisement calling for the death penalty when a woman was viciously attacked while jogging.

Trump was helped along in his deal-making by his political connections: the Trump Organization contributed generously to the gubernatorial campaign of Hugh L. Carey, who was elected and gave the developer the support he needed to go ahead with his projects. Mayor Abraham D. Beame, another recipient of Trump's campaign contributions, also gave him important backing for the Hyatt deal. The Grand Hyatt was completed in 1980 and contained 1,400 rooms, a presidential suite, a ballroom, a shopping arcade, and five restaurants.

After this project, Trump accelerated his pace and purchased the Barbizon-Plaza Hotel and an adjacent apartment house in 1980. In three years the property reportedly increased in value tenfold. He later built Trump Plaza, a cooperative apartment complex worth $125 million, Harrah's hotel-casino in Atlantic City estimated at $250 million, and purchased the New Jersey Generals of the United States Football League for $10 million. Trump has said he would someday like to head his own television network, and hopes to build what would be the tallest building in the world on a Manhattan landfill, as well as a domed sports stadium in New York City – although these projects may have to be put on hold for a long time, or until he can make back the money he has lost.

Of course, a considerably large portion of Trump's money will go to his ex-wife, Ivana, with whom he had previously made a $20 million marriage contract. She contested for more money and they finally settled on $25 million. Trump met Ivana Winkelmayr, a Czechoslovakian fashion model and former Olympic skier, at a party in Montreal in 1975 and reportedly immediately fell in love with her. They were married within a year of meeting by Dr Norman Vincent Peale, and had three children, including Donald Jnr, and Ivanka. Trump made Ivana an executive vice-president in charge of design of the Trump Organization. But in 1990, "The Donald", as Ivana called him, broke up the happy family when he left her for a struggling actress named Marla Maples. It was a very public break-up, with a confrontation between Ivana and Maples on the ski slopes in Aspen, in which the duped wife told the mistress to keep her hands off her husband.

Ivana has done well for herself in the role of jilted wife: she recently wrote a steamy book called *For Love Alone*, which tells a story that sounds amazingly close to her own. The story relates how a Czech model moves to New York and meets a yacht-sailing tycoon, who subsequently leaves her for another woman – a Southern belle. Although Ivana insists that the work is pure fiction, she may be in the hotseat with her ex-husband. Under their settlement agreement, Ivana is forbidden to publish anything "whether fictionalized or not" about their marriage, and Trump may sue.

Since the restructuring of Trump's bank loans, many say he has been exposed as just another developer who paid far more than he should have for his properties. The Plaza hotel, which cost him $400 million, was estimated at a value of $250 million by some real estate experts at the time. But Trump maintains that he did not overpay. Other property developers say Trump has overpaid for nearly everything he has purchased in the last four years. He has lost many of his famous possessions: he sold his $30 million yacht The Trump Princess – the world's largest private yacht, as well as the Trump shuttle airline, his private Boeing 727, half shares in two Atlantic City casinos and several hundred blocks of luxury apartments. Trump is also in the process of selling half of New York's Plaza Hotel as well as half of New York's Grand Hyatt hotel. His biggest worries are yet to come: in June 1993, two mortgages come due for a total of $340 million. Also $115 million in personal debt is due to the banks in mid-1995, as well as an additional $50 million loan the banks extended him to keep afloat. Still, he insists that he's on his way back.

"You'll never see me sitting in the corner sucking my thumb. The name Trump will be hotter than ever," said the former billionaire.

# Alan Bond

They were Australia's folk king and queen. He was the embodiment of the Australian dream, the true to life rags-to-riches entrepreneur who become a hero to the people after bringing his country glory by winning the prestigious yachting trophy, the America's Cup. At the height of his reign of power in the mid-1980s he was worth nearly £1 billion.

But in 1991 Alan Bond, Australia's answer to Donald Trump (*see* page 21) faced bankruptcy court and claimed he had almost nothing left of his fortune. It was the ultimate tale of the multi-millionaire who lived his life to excess, then lost everything when the public's love and admiration turned to envy and mistrust.

Bond was born in 1938 in London and moved with his family to Australia eleven years later. He left school at the age of fifteen because he felt he wasn't being challenged, and took up signpainting as a profession. His goal was to be a millionaire at twenty-one. And he was. At seventeen he married Eileen (her nickname was Red), the daughter of a wool broker named Doozer Hughes. Bond took a loan out from his father-in-law and bought a piece of land in the hills of Perth, on the western coast of Australia. A land boom in the late Sixties left Bond a wealthy man and started him on his way to becoming a millionaire.

"Red" and "Bondy" were a fun-loving, eccentric and attention-grabbing couple who became notorious for their extravagance. In 1987 Bond purchased Van Gogh's Irises at Sotheby's for £30.2 million, which at the time was the largest sum ever paid for a painting. Bond made the purchase anonymously, arousing curiosity as to who the wealthy new owner could be. It was all part of the game, however. And part of Bond's strategy of making outrageous purchases to make people (most importantly bankers) think he was fabulously wealthy.

In truth, Bond's empire was built almost entirely on debts. Early on he adopted the method of financing deals with loans on the equity of his last purchase. In fact, after his much-publicized purchase of Irises, it was revealed that Sotheby's had lent Bond £16 million to purchase the painting, using it as collateral, and that he couldn't repay the money. Eventually, Sotheby's took the painting back. At the height of his success he owned sixty per cent of Australia's television stations, and nearly half the country's beer supply, as well as oil wells, satellites, newspapers and dirigibles (zeppelins). Add to this an entire English village, two private islands, two yachts, ten homes, 95,000 sheep, 10,000 cattle and 300 paintings and one has an idea of the kind of wealth Bond possessed. His wife, Red, would jet off to Singapore on shopping trips after lunch, swathed in diamonds from Bondy's mine.

Bond's charm and great salesmanship were a huge asset in his business dealings. It was said he could sell the cross of St Peter's basilica and persuade the Pope to go along with the deal. Australians gazed at the Bonds with a mixture of despair and affection. To many, Alan Bond was a hero. Especially after he brought the country fame and glory when he won the America's Cup yachting race after his fourth try – a prize that had never been captured by a non-American before.

Besides being a fiercely competitive sportsman, Bond was a shrewd businessman and he knew that a victory in the America's Cup would bring him, in addition to notoriety and respectability, a guarantee on the £20 million in loans he'd taken out from the banks for his most ambitious project to date. Bond was planning on building an entire city – complete with three universities – among the barren sand dunes about thirty miles from Perth. He used the America's Cup as a focal point for his new project, and built a harbour and yacht, the Southern Cross, in his new city.

In 1974, just before Bond's first challenge, the property market in Australia collapsed and the banks wanted their money back. But with Bond being featured in the newspapers every day as Australia's latest sporting celebrity, the banks decided that the political backlash of putting Bond out of business wasn't worth it. "I am going to keep belting away at whoever and whatever stands between us and the cup," he said at the time. In 1983 Bond finally won the America's Cup and became an international celebrity. In Australia he became a god – Prime Minister Bob Hawke wept when he

Alan Bond in happier times.

announced the victory on national television. Many wanted to see Bond knighted, and he received the Order of Australia. A mini-series based on Bondy and Red, The Challenge, was created.

Fortunately for Bond, shortly after his America's Cup victory, banking deregulation began in Australia and the Labour government floated the Australian dollar, making money easier to obtain. Bond went on a spending spree, paying A$1 billion for a major brewery, Castlemaine Tooheys, the largest amount paid for an Australian company at the time. He then purchased the country's most popular television network, Channel Nine, for £600 million, and announced plans to build Bond University. By 1989, Bond owed £4.3 billion and was considered Australia's second richest man.

The old saying "What goes around, comes around", soon came to haunt Bond after he helped topple his old nemesis and competitor Robert Holmes à Court (*see* page 35) by buying out his controlling shares in his holding company, the Bell Group. When Bond was obliged by the federal government to shoulder Bell's debts as well, Australia's "King" of finance nearly went under. It was when he allegedly stabbed his old friend Lonrho Chief Executive Tiny Rowlands in the back by attempting to buy out controlling interest in his company without his knowledge, that Bond dug his own grave. Rowlands, a fierce British competitor, proceeded to publish a ninety-three-page report titled "The Bond Group of Companies: A Financial Analysis by Lonrho Plc", which proceeded to completely destroy Bond's credibility.

The document stated that Bond's companies were technically insolvent and maintained that they were worth about half of what its owner claimed. It also proposed that its debts were three times Bond's figure and that its profits were non-existent. "An investment in Bond Group Companies has been a disaster," it declared. Bond did his best to dismiss the report, calling it rubbish. But the Australian public were not so charmed by him anymore, especially since he had failed to win the America's Cup the year before.

It was feeding time on the Bonds. They made the list of "The 100 Most Appalling People in Australia". Soon Bond's stock prices began to drop and the media joined in on the negative campaign; newspapers ran regular series titled "Bond on the Ropes"; other headlines read "Bond Under the Hammer". He declared there was a conspiracy against him, but still began selling off his companies. He sold Kerry Packer his television network for £85 million in 1990 – the same company he bought off Packer for $450 million three years before. Since then, Bond Brewing has gone into receivership and American creditors have begun legal proceedings in Australia seeking repayment of £281 million worth of debentures. He's been doing his best to stave off bankruptcy. At the time of the stock market crash in October 1987, Alan Bond was believed to be the richest man in Australia with assets of nearly £1 billion.

In September 1991, he was ordered by the courts to repay bank loans of £140 million, believed to be the largest judgment against an individual in Australian legal history. Since then, he and Red have split. And on 14 April 1992, Bond's life of spending finally caught up to him: he was declared bankrupt by Australian courts. His lifestyle will have to undergo great changes. He is not allowed to own a car worth more than £1,100, the luxurious furnishings in his house must be sold, and he cannot apply for credit of more than £230 unless he declares his bankruptcy. He is restricted from becoming a director or manager of a company and must surrender his passport. The only thing Bond will be allowed to keep is his wardrobe full of custom-made suits. But Bond promises a comeback, and he's looking for investors . . .

# Freddie Laker

Sir Freddie Laker was a British folk hero who worked his way up from sweeping airplane hangers at the age of fifteen, to starting his own airline, Skytrain, a no-frills daily service from London to New York. Many say his airline was blown out of the sky by jealous competitors, and in 1982 the company collapsed in a pile of debts. For Sir Freddie it was the death of a long-standing dream.

He was knighted in 1978, at the height of his success with his airline, which offered cheap trans-Atlantic flights and opened up America for thousand of Britons. Laker Airways went belly up in February 1982 owing £270 million. Sir Freddie, who was considered the pioneer of cheap air

Failed Australian media mogul Christopher Skase was declared bankrupt in June 1991 after his debts mounted to more than £37 million. He was formerly chairman of the now failed Qintex group, a media and leisure group which collapsed soon after it failed to take over the American film studio MGM/UA. In 1988, Skase was estimated to be worth more than A$65 million. He was only forty-years-old when he moved into Hollywood to add to his empire of Australian television networks and several luxury tourist resorts. Skase, known to have simple tastes – unlike many of his other millionaire Australian peers – came from humble beginnings. The flamboyant multi-millionaire started out as a financial journalist, but quit his job with the Australian Financial Review to start his own company, Qintex, in 1974. He used his A$15,000 in savings to set up the investment company, which later concentrated on the media, tourism resorts and leisure, and equities and properties. Skase was soon noted for his debonair dress sense and workaholic nature (he regularly worked 100-hour weeks), and after his business took off this rather eccentric entrepreneur purchased a yacht for A$6 million and called it the Mirage III. He decorated it entirely in baby blue – his favourite colour. This meant baby blue wall-to-wall carpeting, baby blue panelling, baby blue marble, and a baby blue banquet table. Before his fall, Skase was eyeing further acquisitions in the US. He had been working in property development in Spain when his company failed, and returned voluntarily to Australia to face charges of two breaches of corporate laws.

travel, fought valiantly to save his airline, but after months of negotiations the rescue attempt failed. The announcement that the ten-year-old airline consisting of seventeen aircraft was going under left passengers and holiday-makers stranded all over the world, and some Skytrain aircraft leaving Britain were recalled in mid-flight.

The public support for Sir Freddie was tremendous; a "Save Laker" fund was started and people called him asking where they could send money and what they could do to help: thousands of pounds were sent in. He was a passionate believer in the idea of setting up a cheap and easily available air network for everyone, and the people liked and respected him for this. His was the classic rags-to-riches story, which unfortunately ended in rags.

The son of a scrap dealer and a cleaning woman, Laker started his first business at the age of twenty-six – when he opened an aircraft spare parts company based on his savings of £240. An investment of £38,000 by a Scottish banker let the young entrepreneur expand into buying a dozen Halton aircraft (converted Halifax bombers). Later these aircraft helped get supplies into Berlin when it was under a Soviet blockade, and Aviation Traders was subsequently responsible for nearly twelve per cent of the food the city dwellers received over the next thirteen months. Even then, Laker wasn't making much in the way of profit and was known for thinking big and trusting that work would eventually come in to cover costs and make more money.

After twelve years of running the company and earning the reputation of being willing to fly anywhere, he sold the company for £800,000. Soon after he joined the board of British United Airways and became their managing director with an annual salary of £5,000 a year. In 1965, after a public row with BUA chairman Sir Miles Wyatt, he left the company and started Laker Airways. The company started off with three planes bought with £215,000 of his savings and the rest from bank loans.

When Laker tried to move into the trans-Atlantic market, however, he ran into opposition from aviation authorities as well as other carriers. Before Skytrain began its flights in 1977, British Airways, TWA and Pan Am were secretly meeting to plan his downfall. After a five-year fight, Sir Freddie had gained enough public backing so that Skytrain was born. His idea was to operate an air service that was much like a train, where people only had to turn up at the airport without booking and could take off at a cheap fare. He was finally given permission by the US Department of Transportation in June 1977 to undercut the cheapest trans-Atlantic fares by at least £80. When he received this approval, Air India, Iran Air and El Al – all airlines which operate between London and New York – joined in with the other airlines in a series of secret meetings to knock Laker out of the sky.

As soon as Skytrain went into operation it was an immediate success. On the inaugural flight to Los Angeles, Laker shook hands and talked to the passengers, and they told him that without Skytrain they would have never been able to afford to fly to the USA. "We treated the people like real human beings. We didn't treat them like cattle, we didn't treat them like passengers; we treated them like people," said Laker at the time.

On a high, he borrowed hundreds of millions of dollars to buy new aircraft for his fleet and run a European Skytrain service he was planning. A year after Laker launched Skytrain, he was awarded a knighthood – the greatest symbol of acceptance he could have achieved. The ex-Prime Minister Margaret Thatcher was one of his biggest backers and fans. But eventually the opposition from the major airlines and the recession defeated him and his loans turned into heavy burdens when interest rates rose and the exchange rate plummeted. The final blow was given when Pan Am lowered its prices to match those of Laker's fleet. Laker Airways collapsed on 5 February 1982. In August 1985 he accepted an $8 million peace offer from British Airways and other airlines who he accused of allegedly conspiring to put him out of business and prevent him from starting up again. This cleared the way for the privatization of BA.

Since the failure of Laker Airways, Sir Freddie has tried his hand at running a package tour operation, inventing a magnetic game for passengers to play with on flights, and at the age of seventy he has recently started Laker Airways again with the aim of flying holiday-makers between the United States and the Bahamas at cheap rates and eventually moving back into the British/American market operating low-cost trans-Atlantic flights.

Once as patriotic as they come, Laker now says he avoids Britain like the plague: "The way I was treated by the government and the British travel trade, I don't owe England a thing. The country would have to change a hell of a lot for me to want to go galloping back there. I'm appreciated here in America. The Brits don't appreciate anyone."

# Ivar Kreuger

Swedish born millionaire Ivar Kreuger was known as the "Match King" and once owned the world's largest monopoly. During the 1920s he was sole owner or controlled the supply of three-quarters of the world's matches. But just a few years later, Kreuger killed himself with a pistol, with little left of his $650 million fortune after squandering or losing most of it.

Kreuger was trained as an engineer in his native Sweden, then travelled the world before returning there to start a construction company. He soon became successful and began building throughout Europe, then branched out into banking and film financing. After finding that he could get supplies of phosphorous and potash for the manufacturing of matches, when others could not, he decided to go into the business and in 1915 he started his own match company.

By 1917 he was raking in the profits, had taken over his competitors and was in control of the Swedish match industry. Eventually he moved into France, Yugoslavia, Turkey, Eastern Europe, and South and Central America where he also monopolized the industry. Kreuger was an eccentric businessman, however, and took to compulsively layering his empire with mysterious companies where he could launder funds. He always had a great deal for the investor with higher interest than anyone else could offer, and when rumours surfaced that Kreuger was having problems with his businesses, he would purposely overpay his taxes by $150,000 to make others think he was still a very wealthy man. As Robert Maxwell (*see* page 8) later did, Kreuger would pretend to take phone calls from world leaders such as Stalin, to impress his waiting visitors. He began putting together more and more deals, but his companies weren't making enough money to pay the huge dividends he promised, so the "Match King" began forging notes. One note he forged from the Italian government was for $143 million.

In 1931, Kreuger suffered a stroke, presumably caused by the incredible stress he was feeling by trying to juggle his fraudulent deals. Finally, on 12 March 1932, he put an end to his life with a shotgun. Although he considered himself a ruined man, he was still worth $200 million at the time of his death – despite squandering hundreds of millions of dollars and losing a hundred million more.

# Robert Holmes à Court

The late Robert Holmes à Court, one of a series of Australian entrepreneurs who lost nearly everything in the stock market crash of 1987, is remembered as a businessman who took huge but carefully calculated risks. He was known as the Lone Ranger and was once feared by his rivals as one of the shrewdest and most ruthless corporate raiders of the 1980s: he knew how to manipulate the market so that he could profit immensely from placing major companies in tenuous positions. The aloof Holmes à Court was once considered the richest man in Australia with a wealth estimated at £650 million ($1.4 billion) and became a symbolic figure of the 1980s international business scene which featured financiers who used debt to build their fortunes.

Named the "great acquirer" by the media, this carefully spoken lawyer owned newspapers, radio and television stations in Australia and later took over the Associated Communications Corporation in Britain – ousting its chairman Lord Grade. Holmes à Court was also a large shareholder in various international concerns, including Texaco, Standard Chartered Bank, Pioneer Concrete, and Australia's biggest public company, BHP. His flagship company was the Bell Group, which he was later forced to sell to his arch-rival, fellow businessman Alan Bond (*see* page 26), when the stock market crash erased sixty per cent of the company's worth in one day. After the crash, he saw his fortune reduced at the rate of nearly $8 million a day for a time. Unlike Bond and his other compatriots, however, Holmes à Court did not concentrate on one specific industry but rather he specialized in special situations wherever he could find them. His success was a result of the trading skills and market wizardry he honed over two decades in the business world.

Born in South Africa, he attended the elite Michaelhouse boarding school, then left to study agricultural science in New Zealand. He later migrated to Australia and set up a law firm in Perth after studying law at the University of Western Australia. It was there that he met his future wife, Janet, with whom he later had four children. A former classmate recalled how even then he was plotting how to takeover BHP. While

Australian media magnate Robert Holmes à Court.

in Perth, a conservative, isolated city at the time, Holmes à Court devised his strategy for the takeovers and raids he later used to surprise the business world. He was an Anglophile who was proud of his ancestry, which predated the Norman conquest of England in 1066, and his ties to the Baron of Heytesbury. Collecting vintage cars was one of his passions, and his collection was used in the film The Great Gatsby. His scheme was to identify likely targets, buy shares and wait for the market's response to his purchase of a "strategic" stake, then sell all the shares on a profit or put in a bid. He nearly always walked away with a huge profit. A failed bid he made for Rolls-Royce in 1980 still resulted in a A$1 million profit for him.

In 1970, Holmes à Court had succeeded in his first step towards making a million dollars when he bought a company called West Australian Worsted and Woollen Mills and used it to move on a nickel claim at the right time. After placing one million Woollen Mills shares on the market, he raised A$1.5 million. He later used his companies the Bell Group and Bell Resources to perform daring raids on some of the biggest and most established companies in Australia. He targeted the airline and transport group Ansett, the *Herald* and *Weekly Times*, and shocked the board of ACC when he moved on the troubled company in 1982. The company owned the box-office hit On Golden Pond and the rights to a portfolio of Beatles songs. Holmes à Court later sold the rights to the tunes to Michael Jackson for $50 million. Holmes à Court later described the scene in the boardroom: "I called a board meeting and I said, 'Lord Grade has offered to sell me shares. I am prepared to buy them, but these are my conditions. Number one is that I want to be appointed chairman of the board right now. If I am, then I will provide £20 million unsecured to save the company from receivership. My offer is open until the end of the day'." The board gave in to his demands. Once Holmes à Court made it onto the board of directors he would usually entrench himself there.

His game plan, however, only lasted until the stock market crash in 1987 and his dream of building an empire that included Britain, the United States and Australia was shattered. The Bell Group, with assets consisting mostly of equities and shareholdings financed by borrowings, fared miserably that fateful October. In one day, Holmes à Court's fortune was slashed by two-thirds to A$550 million. Despite this giant loss, he started investing once again and shortly before he died he had purchased thirteen theatres in London's West End and a stake in Andrew Lloyd Webber's Really Useful Group.

The man who died of a heart attack at the age of fifty-three in September 1990, was one of Australia's most respected art collectors and thoroughbred horse breeders. He was somewhat of a social loner and was disparaging of his brasher counterparts, such as Alan Bond. Publicly he was a one-man show, though he kept a closely knit team of advisers who kept his numerous deals in motion. The financier shunned publicity – "I'm not public property and I'm not running for public office," he would say – and claimed blue blood through his father, who was related to the fourth Lord Heytesbury. He used the Heytesbury name for his family company and horse stud farm where he lived with his wife until his death.

# Hunt brothers

The legendary Hunt family fortune – one of the largest in the world – collapsed in 1980 when their attempt to corner the world's silver market failed and they lost $1.5 billion in the process. It was considered the largest personal financial reversal in American history. In 1986, the family wealth foundered again when their key company, Penrod Drilling, went under and the Hunts had to file for protection under Chapter 11 bankruptcy laws to stave off their creditors and prevent the banks from foreclosing on their prime remaining assets: their gas, oil and real estate. The Texas billionaires' fortune plummeted from $8 billion in 1980 to $2 billion in 1986, and many believe the family has been lowered even further since then to become mere multi-millionaires.

Nelson Bunker Hunt, aged sixty-six, and the flamboyant head of the clan, once said that a man who knew how much he was worth was not worth much. Those words later came back to haunt him as he and his two brothers,

Herbert, aged sixty-three, and Lamar, aged sixty, and three sisters, Margaret, Caroline and Hassie, struggled to retain their immense wealth. They inherited the legacy of their legendary father, H.L. Hunt, a gambler, womanizer, and wildcatter who invested his poker winnings in some large east Texas oil wells and made a fortune. Yet, even with his millions, this oilman still took a sandwich to the office in a brown paper bag for lunch. The Hunt brothers took the fortune when their father died at the age of eighty-five and multiplied it considerably when Bunker discovered a mammoth oil field in Libya in 1961. They then lost at least $4 billion when the value of their investments in land, silver, crude oil and sugar collapsed.

The arch-conservative family was the most notorious of the Dallas super-rich, and many residents there felt that the brothers had become arrogant and aloof, though they still kept their private telephone number listed in the directory and Bunker Hunt dressed simply and flew tourist class. Yet, the people of Texas did not want to see the empire fail and have the family take their jobs with them. In 1986, the Hunt family found themselves embroiled in bankruptcy and other court proceedings and were fighting off twenty-three bankers whom they owed more than $1.6 billion in outstanding loans. Still, it was not the first time the billionaires had come under fire. The brothers were found guilty in 1980 by a New York jury of conspiring with various Arabs to corner the silver market between June 1979 and March 1980. The judge ordered them to pay $130 million in damages to Minpeco, a company controlled by the Peruvian government. They lost heavily in the silver market at the time and blamed the Hunts for their misfortune – and the jury agreed with them.

Minpeco alleged that the brothers had been planning their coup in the silver market for at least a year before they put it into effect. During the winter of 1974-75, Bunker Hunt met with two commodity brokers and a Pakistani bullion dealer in London to seek advice as to how they could permanently raise the price of silver. The dealer, Haji Ashraf, a dubious figure who sold tens of millions of ounces of silver allegedly smuggled out of India to markets in New York and Chicago, told Hunt that the way to do it was to involve the Arabs, thereby giving the commodity the cache of being recognized as that of the oil sheiks; they were already holding the West to ransom at this time through OPEC. Hunt had decided that silver was the commodity of the future since demand had begun to outstrip its production in the early 1960s, and bought about fifty million ounces of the metal at $3 an ounce. The price of silver almost immediately rose to over $6 an ounce, but then dropped to $4 an ounce. After reaching a high of over $50 an ounce during their scam, the price of the metal dropped to $15 and the Hunt family was left with huge losses. By 1986, silver was worth only $5.50 an ounce.

When the bottom fell out of the Hunts' scheme, Paul Volcker, chairman of the Federal Reserve Board, recognized a shaken Wall Street and persuaded a group of banks to bail out the former billionaires with a $1.1 billion loan. As security, the Texans put up one million acres of ranchland in Texas, Montana and Oklahoma, 700 thoroughbred horses, four million acres of grazing land in Australia, and a collection of ancient coins and other valuable objects. They even sold Herbert's Greek and Roman statues, Lamar's Rolex watch, and a portrait of Bunker and his son in order to extricate themselves from their troubles and avoid a congressional investigation. Although the billionaires had been suspected of manipulating the market, the US Justice Department never brought criminal charges against them, instead leaving it to the individual investors to seek compensation through the civil courts. The case Minpéco subsequently brought against the Hunts lasted seven years and involved a team of nine lawyers who acted for the Peruvian company and took 200 depositions in eight countries and subpoenaed more than a million documents, including telephone records, credit card receipts, hotel and flight records and bank files from cities in the US and Europe. From these records the lawyers planned to prove that the Hunt brothers had taken part in a series of meetings throughout 1979 and part of 1980 with several Arab sheiks all over the world to plot their scheme. Though the Hunts claimed that the meetings were only social, the jurors believed the Minpeco assertion that they were proof that an international conspiracy had been working to rig the silver market. A week after Bunker Hunt attended a dinner party in August 1979 hosted by a prominent Saudi real estate developer and racehorse owner named Mahmoud Fustok, the Arab purchased several million ounces of silver.

The eldest Hunt had met Fustok and Naji Nahas, a Lebanese merchant, at the Prix de l'Arc de Triomphe – Europe's richest horse race. Bunker presumably attended the

The billionaire Hunt brothers, who attempted to corner the world silver market.

event as part of his search for Arab investors to join his silver scheme. Previously, he had made his pitch to the Shah of Iran and King Faisal, who had both refused. He nearly persuaded Filippino President Ferdinand Marcos to take part in the conspiracy by way of a complicated three-way barter deal, but the plan fell through. In addition to Fustok and Nahas, Hunt also recruited three other Arabs: Ali bin Mussalem, a confidant of King Fahd of Saudi Arabia; Mohammed Aboud al Amoudi, a Saudi merchant; and Mohammed Affara, a London-based financier. The group founded a joint company called International Metals Investment Company, which was created to buy silver. By 1980, the business was worth nearly $16 billion and the Hunts held a third of the world's silver and seventy-four per cent of the US silver market. The price of silver spiralled to $52.50, and investors started to scramble for a chunk of the metal. Minpeco could not buy enough silver to meet their contracts and had to buy from the Hunts.

Minpeco later proved through its lawyers that the meetings between the Hunt brothers and the Arab investors took place at the same time that important trades occurred in the silver market. Bunker Hunt tried to pass off the rise in the price of the metal by attributing it to investors who were worried about the world events such as the hostage crisis in Iran, and the Soviet invasion of Afghanistan. While the trial was going on, concerned American authorities placed strict controls on silver buying and with long queues forming outside silver dealers, the price of the metal plunged to $10 an ounce. The Hunts lost more than $2 billion and were rescued from their predicament by the federal government only when they threatened to take several important broking firms down with them. Despite the debacle, the family was still worth more than $3 billion.

It was in 1983 when the oil price crashed that the Texas billionaires began to see their fortune diminish and decided to divide up their assets, with the brothers taking Placid and the silver debt, and the sisters taking the gas leases and real estate, concentrating on building elegant hotels and office complexes in Dallas and Beverly Hills. Their troubles grew worse when their company Penrod Drilling, the second largest off-shore drilling fleet in the world, collapsed, and Placid Oil, the cornerstone of the Hunt empire and one of the largest privately owned American oil companies, defaulted on its bank loans in 1985. The brothers were ordered by a Texas judge to file for Chapter 11 bankruptcy protection from their creditors in order to avoid foreclosure of their prime assets. They allegedly sought to buy time and reorganize Placid by filing in Louisiana, where the law is notably easier, instead of in Dallas. The judge then ordered the Hunts to file in Dallas within seven days. The banks, burned from dealing with the Hunt brothers over sugar losses, wanted more collateral and higher interest from the family. The Hunts wanted a grace period to repay their debt so that they could develop oilfields in the Dutch sector of the North Sea and the Green Canyon field in the Gulf of Mexico. Bunker Hunt, who liked to boast that "no bank ever lost money dealing with the Hunts", was cornered. So the family did what their father would have done; they bought time by suing the banks for conspiring to destroy their business, then sued them again when the bankers tried to foreclose. The claims reached $14 billion. Bankers were concerned about the plan to develop the new oilfields because, given the depressed oil prices at the time, the company had to turn to unproven high-technology in order to make a profit. Placid wanted to use a new floating production system that would allow it to operate in waters deeper than normally possible to pump in.

For a while, it looked as though the brothers might emerge from the mess and still be worth a cool $1 billion. But, since the judgment in the silver suit against the Hunts, they face several more law suits and could lose everything. Two suits for $500 million have already been filed against the family on behalf of 17,000 small investors in the silver market during the Hunts' buying spree. "The Minpeco case establishes the fact that there was a conspiracy," said Herbert Deutsch, the lawyer handling the case. "My case alone will kill them."

# Asil Nadir

Asil Nadir, the Cyprus-born entrepreneur who was once Britain's thirty-fifth richest man, is now facing charges by the government of stealing more than £42 million from his companies, including Polly Peck International, and has endured a reversal of fortune on a scale that few in the history of British commerce have suffered.

Nadir was an obsessive money-maker and a workaholic who transformed a small rag-trade company he named Polly Peck into the world's third-largest fruit trader in one decade, with profits of £160 million. At his peak, he boasted that he was probably worth $1 billion. But in a matter of weeks, the share prices of his company plummeted to less than half and in six hours of stock market trading, Nadir's fortune had plunged by £165 million after Britain's Serious Fraud Office announced it was investigating Polly Peck and its

chairman. This was the same company which had emerged
as the world's best share of the Eighties, and saw the most
dramatic rise in the value of its shares in that decade –
anyone who invested £1,000 in his company in 1980 would
find it worth £1.2 million nearly ten years later. In 1990, a
bankruptcy petition was brought against him by his own
stockbrokers insisting on payment of £3.6 million worth of
Polly Peck shares he had purchased.

The success of his company convinced banks to lend
him money to expand his businesses as well as furnish
himself with all the trappings of a wealthy tycoon. His
assets included a 2,000-acre farm in Leicestershire, a Bel-
gravia estate in Wilton Crescent, houses in Turkey and
Cyprus, a stable of race-horses and a collection of French
furniture and paintings. These days, however, his shares
are virtually worthless and Nadir is almost certainly broke,
left with few assets. After paying his receivers and creditors the money he owes them – estimated at £100 million – Nadir could beat William Stern as Britain's largest
bankrupt.

Nadir had always been a loner and somewhat of an
outsider. His departure from the financial scene in Britain
had little impact on the City, London's financial district. Still,
he was not unpopular and was considered a gracious, affable
man who contributed regularly to lesser-known charities: he
gave £5 million to the Spastic Society before his collapse.
And despite his good looks and charm, he wasn't a playboy,
but rather at the age of forty-seven, had cultivated the
image of a sober father who wanted to protect Britain's
architectural heritage. He was always elusive, even to his
friends and family: his younger son, Sirhan, had to make an
appointment with his father's secretary to see him. He was
described by a former business colleague as being charming
and mercurial: "He's bright, with fantastic business vision,
he's charismatic, very quick-minded with an interesting
sense of humour." Other former associates said he could
be volatile, firing and hiring senior executives in a desperate
attempt to prove that Polly Peck's future wasn't dominated
by him.

The self-made tycoon, whose name in Turkish means rare
(Asil) and noble (Nadir), was born in Lafka, a Cypriot copper
mining town, in May 1941 to an energetic and ambitious
father named Irfan Nadir who had taught himself English

and worked as a translator for a mining company before starting an ice cream business, along with a supermarket, a bus service, a restaurant and a newspaper business – sending his son off at the age of six to sell newspapers he could hardly carry. His father, Nadir has said, gave him a good practical grounding in business. "I worked so hard, school was a holiday," he said. When war broke out in his homeland in the mid-Fifties, Irfan Nadir's businesses were attacked and he lost everything, prompting him to move his family to London's East End in 1963, where he immediately set up a business in the rag trade because it was an easy business to gain entry to with little capital. Meanwhile, Asil Nadir stayed behind in Turkey where he was attending the University of Istanbul, studying economics. Those times were hard for Nadir, who says he experienced hunger. He started a pop group called the Asils, of which he was the lead singer, in order to help fund his education, but left before earning a degree to join his family in London. There, he went into the same business as his father – selling rags. He eventually started his own cash-and-carry clothing company in 1967 which he called Wearwell when he realized that controlling a market was crucial to making money.

While in his twenties, he married Ayesha, a former Turkish beauty queen who he later divorced then married and divorced again. The second time they married he bought her a wooden palace on the Bosphorus which was once owned by an Ottoman pasha. He called in former US secretary of state Henry Kissinger, who is an expert in antiques, to help him furnish his mansion. After divorcing Ayesha again, he met Narin Ferdi, the thirty-two-year-old daughter of a Turkish-Cypriot banker to whom he later announced his engagement. But his business would always come first for him. When asked if he was passionate about his first wife, he replied: "I'm only passionate about business." Still, his family and his old friends in Cyprus were also important to him.

Nadir's business swiftly began improving and by the early Seventies his company took off when he set up a clothing factory on a Nicosia industrial estate after the government appealed to expatriates to help their ailing economy; profits were about £1 million a year. After noting the potential of the quickly growing Iraqi and Libyan economies, he began exporting clothing in bulk to the Middle East using his Muslim connections. By 1980 his company was valued at £12 million, after having survived the 1974-75 property crash (Nadir had bought up large parcels of Commercial Road in London, where his business was located). Nadir traded on his Turkish connections to build a close relationship with the government of Turkey; President Turget Ozal came to his aid when his company had trouble and appealed to Margaret Thatcher to help Polly Peck survive. After earning a Queen's Award for Exports in the 1980s, Nadir returned home a hero. He is still considered a champion of the people there, though he is a scoundrel to his former stockholders in The City. To his fellow Cypriots, he is the king, their saviour, the man who brought them jobs when they had none, and confidence in themselves when it was lacking. Some Turkish-Cypriots regarded themselves happily as citizens of "Nadirland", while Greek-Cypriots used the term disparagingly.

His next venture was to build a cardboard box factory in Cyprus to help solve the problem of sending the island's rich fruit crop to market. The business, started with the support of the Cypriot Government, sent Polly Peck's profits soaring from nearly nothing to £9 million in 1982, with profits doubling every year. Many investors and financial journalists were sent off to find out how Nadir's business had scored such astonishing profits by a mere cardboard box company, but their suspicions were never substantiated, despite an audit of Polly Peck. Before Nadir moved into the produce market in Cyprus, Turkey was exporting only a fifth of the millions of tons of citrus fruit, grapes and tomatoes it grew, whereas Spain exported two-thirds of its produce. His company became number one in the world in trading pineapples and provided crucial financial support for Cyprus. Still, he was criticized for his successes and for being too British. He blamed the disapproval on the Greek-Cypriots who he thought were instigating suspicions in the press against him. He denied exploiting the workers and defended his control of his company.

And Nadir did not stop at fruit. He soon built a colour television factory in Turkey, along with hotels and leisure complexes and a Turkish mineral water bottling plant. Annual sales rose to nearly £2 billion. To gain the

political influence in Turkey that he never had, he spent
£100 million to buy up several newspapers there as well
as its main weekly magazine. His company, Polly Peck,
went on to take control of Sansui electronics, the Pizza
Hut franchise in Turkey, and paid £550 million for the
respected Del Monte fresh fruit company in the US. For
years he withstood allegations about the legitimacy of his
company, and in the City many expressed doubts about
Polly Peck and wondered how it could make so much
more profit than other companies selling fresh fruit. The
suspicions culminated in 1989 when it was announced that
both the Stock Exchange's insider-trading group and Inland
Revenue investigators had been examining suspicious Polly
Peck share sales overseas. When the Serious Fraud Office
and the Metropolitan Police confirmed that they had confiscated documents from Nadir's Mayfair London offices,
his company's market value dropped by half. They also
began investigating mysterious deals with secretive Swiss
companies which allegedly controlled his business operations.

Shortly after the investigation was revealed, Nadir offered
to buy all the shares in his company that he did not already
own and take the company private at an estimated cost of
£1.5 billion. After Polly Peck shares jumped to 450p, their
highest ever, with this announcement, Nadir announced
that he had dropped the plan, leading to an official rebuke
by the Stock Exchange authorities and throwing a question
of credibility onto the tycoon. Since then, Polly Peck has
collapsed as more than £560 million was knocked off its
shares. In December 1990 he was charged with eighteen
offenses of theft and false accounting involving more than
£25 million. He was arrested by the Serious Fraud Office
shortly thereafter when he flew back to Heathrow Airport.
He was released on £3.5 million bail after spending several
nights in custody. Nadir is also facing a bankruptcy hearing
filed by creditors.

The contents of his luxurious offices located in London have
since been auctioned off, including his George III mahogany
desk worth nearly £40,000 and many other antiques, paintings, tapestries and other *objects d'art*. The sale was ordered
by the company's administrators and was expected to raise
£3 million towards the company's £1.3 billion debt. Nadir
apparently wanted to bring some English country elegance

to Polly Peck's headquarters office, which contained two watercolours by Turner valued at £280,000.

# Ernest Saunders

The name Ernest Saunders cannot be uttered without the word Guinness coming to mind: he was tried and convicted on twelve out of thirteen counts of fraud involving illegally buying up shares of the company he worked for during a takeover bid so that its share prices would spiral. Prosecutors at his trial said it was his ambition to become head of a world-class company that led to "his greed for money and power . . . not caring about members of the public who might be cheated by his scheme."

"Deadly Ernest", as he was dubbed by the brewery workers in Dublin for his ruthlessness, has seen his life change dramatically from the time he was making £375,000 as chairman of Guinness, makers and marketers of fine Irish stout and spirits. After a four-year wait for his trial, Saunders, fifty-six, was found guilty of share-rigging and given a five-year sentence. He did less than a year of his time, however. His sentence was cut in half after the judge was informed by expert witnesses that the former Guinness boss suffered from a degenerative brain condition likened to Alzheimer's Disease. Since his release, Saunders's condition has improved greatly, leading to speculation that he might have exaggerated his symptoms so that his sentence would be reduced. He now claims that it was possibly a "cocktail" of tranquilizers and sleeping tablets that caused him to suffer bouts of depression and memory loss as well as confusion and disorientation. A sleeping tablet that he used has since been taken off the market.

Convicted of theft, false accounting and breaches of the Companies Act, the former executive now makes a once-a-fortnight trip to his local dole office and is looking for a job as well as carrying out market research for a number of projects he is considering. He was dumped by Guinness when the scandal broke. Despite having agreed with the company that he would step down from his position as long as he remained on salary and Guinness met his legal costs in fighting the allegations, he was fired less than a week later, after recovering from a mild coronary attack, and denied any legal assistance. Since his release from Ford Open Prison in June 1991, Saunders has had a few job offers but said he did not feel well enough at the time to go back to work. There has been speculation that he may be reconciled with his wife, Carole, who is legally separated from him and has been living in Switzerland where she is recovering from two nervous breakdowns she suffered when the Guinness sensation hit the newsstands. She has always maintained that her husband is innocent. Saunders insists that he was a scapegoat for the famous brewing company which brought him to work for them in 1981 because of his background in marketing, and is bitter that they ditched him shortly after he pulled off the biggest deal in the company's history. During his trial he said that there had been a "Get rid of Ernie bandwagon." He is angry that Guinness has been allowed to keep the billions of dollars it made from the allegedly illegal deal which landed him in jail. It is widely accepted that Saunders saved Guinness from a fateful decline; share prices increased six-fold and the company's capitalization rose from £90 million in 1981 to £4 billion in 1987, when he was fired.

Saunders has had to sell his family mansion, Knoll House, in Penn, Buckinghamshire for £700,000 – half of which went to his wife. A quarter of the money was spent on legal fees and the other quarter was used to buy a small house with a garden in Putney where he lives with his three children, Jo, aged twenty-six, Jamie, twenty-five, and John, nineteen. It was Jamie that wrote the book on his father's predicament, "*Nightmare: The Ernest Saunders Story*", which later became a bestseller. The family lived off the money the book made them for a short while, but now Saunders says, "I have no money whatsoever." His legal fees cost him £400,000. His living standard is a far cry from the time he would go everywhere in a chauffeured limousine, owned property in Switzerland and France, and was director of the sponsored soccer club Queen's Park Rangers. Although he cries poverty, Saunders is probably the only person at his dole office who carries around a portable telephone.

Born Ernest Walter Schleyer in Vienna on 21 October 1935, his family later changed its name to Saunders after it fled from the Nazis to England in 1938. There he attended St

Paul's School, London and upon graduating from Emmanuel College, Cambridge, he took his first marketing job with the American company 3M. In 1964 he married Carole and took a job with the Beecham Group conducting worldwide marketing. It was after working for the food giant Nestlé in Switzerland as a product director that he was head-hunted by an American company to head up Guinness. Saunders helped strengthen the company by successfully giving a new image to an old product, while concentrating on its brewing facilities and selling off dozens of companies it had acquired, quadrupling the share price. The new company boss, however, had one problem: he hated the taste of Guinness stout. But, for the sake of image, he would often be seen drinking it and devised ways in which he could get by with consuming only token quantities. Once, a photographer caught him dumping his pint into the shrubbery.

He also assisted in the company's takeover of the Martins newsagents chain in 1984, Bell's Whisky in 1985, and the Scottish company Distillers in 1986 for £2.7 billion – the largest bid in Britain at the time. Saunders angered the Scottish establishment when he refused to keep on Sir Thomas Risk as the chairman for Distillers. Shortly after the sale of the company, Olivier Roux, the Guinness finance director whom Saunders had brought in, sent a letter to his company's solicitors implicating Saunders in a share support operation during the Distillers bid. It alleged that Guinness had been buying its own shares illegally during the bid to push up its share price, which would have made the Guinness offer worth more since it was offering its own shares in exchange for Distillers shares. Saunders maintains that he knew nothing about the financial operation of the company and that he left the Distillers bid to others with whom he worked. Roux, however, said he found Saunders's protestations "laughable" and insisted that his boss was involved in all aspects of the bid. Saunders also repudiates suggestions that he suffered a mental breakdown after realizing that the share-support operation could have broken the law, and that he started lying about his involvement as a cover-up. Of the original 107 charges levelled against the seven people implicated in the Guinness scandal, forty-five of these were against Saunders. Some of his fellow defendants walked free, including former director of Morgan Grenfell Roger Seelig, on grounds of poor health. The others, Sir Jack Lyons, Gerald Ronson, Anthony

Parnes, were convicted. Thomas Ward is awaiting extradition and Ephraim Margulies was not charged.

Saunders has been described as a difficult, arrogant and manipulative boss who was a workaholic, ambitious and a bore. Many former employees paint a picture of an insensitive employer who had little time for niceties, and didn't inspire much loyalty. He admits now that he made mistakes: "I was so focused on the Herculean task to be achieved, that I am now only too willing to believe that I did not spend enough time on the niceties of life. I am the sort of person who always thought that the results should speak for themselves. It is quite possible people found me tough or cold. I was a machine." He was the ultimate company man, and neglected his family. It wasn't until the scandal broke and the trial loomed near that his family became close and he got to know his kids, Saunders admits.

He says that his "colleagues" in prison were amazed that he had ended up with what he called an "enforced holiday" – inside in other words – and hadn't even made any money for himself out of the whole business. "I was apparently considered the dunce of the academy," he says.

He maintains that he was singled out for punishment because he was never part of the City establishment. He argues that this made him a target to be used as a scapegoat by the British government before the 1987 election to prove that it was not soft on City deception. At the time, stories of insider trading were spreading throughout the City; Ivan Boesky (see page 14), the American arbitrageur who had links with Guinness, was fined $100 million for insider trading in the United States.

Now Saunders says he doesn't want to work for anyone else ever again: "I want to be a part proprietor, not just a manager. I spent so many years making, quite frankly, a great deal of money for other people, that I want to do it for myself this time."

The expense of clearing his name – which was most important to Saunders – swallowed up most of his resources. He took to wearing worn suits, eating candy bars in court, and taking buses and the tube to bring home his indignation at an innocent being accused of crime. The prosecution came under fire for dragging the trial out by demanding repeated remand hearings. It was four years before Saunders went to trial, and mounting public concern regarding the delays brought the

former Guinness boss sympathy from the people. He began
to receive letters from strangers expressing their objections
to the way he was being treated, and Saunders took strength
from this. As a result of the Guinness affair, as well as the
recent Barlow Clowes and Blue Arrow trials, two of the judges
involved have called for a reform of the system, and respected
lawyers have publicly criticized the system. Saunders refuses
to admit that he did anything wrong and may bring the issue
up with the European Court of Justice.

- chapter three -

# HIGH LIVING

*T*hinking yourself above others will eventually bring about your *downfall. Ignoring the law and dictating to those around you will, at the end of the day, only serve to alienate those people.*

## Leona and Harry Helmsley

Leona Helmsley, the Queen of Mean who owned a fortune in New York hotels, once told her housekeeper: "We don't

> French car tycoon Andre Citroen liked to think big. During the Paris Exposition in 1922 he had an airplane spell out his name in white smoke above the fair, while Citroen cars all over the city gave citizens rides to the fair. Many of his fellow French citizens were outraged by his display, but when his sales rocketed, Citroen quickly came up with another gimmick – he had his name lit up on the Eiffel Tower with 25,000 electric bulbs. Eventually however, Citroen spent all his money, mainly on women and gambling and died flat broke. He used to plan on losing at the gaming tables for publicity reasons – up to 13,000 francs at a time.

pay taxes. Only the little people pay taxes." Three years later this statement was to help land the woman everyone loved to hate in jail for tax evasion. The hotel magnate apparently forgot that she was not exempt from paying $1.7 million in taxes just because she considered herself royalty.

"We did it for the little people," said one juror after her conviction in a New York courtroom in 1989. According to investigators, who were helped by over 100 former Helmsley employees, the couple had disguised $4 million of personal spending as business expenditure. After she was convicted of five counts of tax evasion, filing false returns and conspiring to defraud the taxman, the New York City tabloids went crazy with headlines like "For hotel queen, a pen-house, maybe?", and "Rhymes with Rich . . ." with a picture of Helmsley next to it.

The story first broke after a disgruntled employee told the New York Post in 1985 that the Helmsleys were claiming improvements to their $8 million twenty-eight-room Jacobean-style Connecticut mansion as business expenditures so they could deduct it from their taxes. After a year of investigation, the paper splashed the headline: "Helmsley Scam Bared", and threw some cold water on the couple's good fortunes. The paper reported that millions of dollars in renovation bills were falsified as business expenses and charged to Manhattan office buildings.

Her lawyer used the defence that she was "a tough bitch" who incurred such fear among her staff that they independently resorted to faking invoices to minimize the time they had to spend in her company.

Despite legal appeals and tearful pleas to the judge to stay out of jail due to ailing health ("Jail would be a death sentence," she said), Helmsley was sent to prison in April 1992 at the age of seventy-one and became inmate number 15113–054. She will trade a life of luxury for a shared cell at the Federal Medical Centre in Lexington, Kentucky where she will not find room service – inmates are expected to clean their rooms and make their own beds as well as join the prison workforce of laundry, sewing or grounds-keeping duty. Helmsley left her Park Lane Hotel in Manhattan by limousine and flew to what will be her new home for the next four years in her personal Boeing 727. Her eighty-three year-old husband, Harry, worth $5 billion, escaped prosecution because he was ruled mentally incompetent to stand trial.

Billionaire hotel magnates Leona and Harry Helmsley.

> **Barbara Hutton's life changed on her twenty-first birthday in 1930. She inherited $20 million ($148 million today) from her grandfather, Frank Woolworth, a tycoon who owned the five and dime chain-store which bears his name. Hutton spent most of her fortune on her husbands – all seven of them, including the actor Cary Grant.**

The woman who launched an advertising campaign which featured her as the "Queen" standing guard at the Helmsley Hotels, came from a humble background. She was born Leona Mindy Rosenthal in Marbletown, just north of New York City to Polish immigrant parents. She was brought up in Brooklyn, and although she claims to have attended college and worked as a successful model, there are no records to be found of either of these achievements. Helmsley later changed her name to Roberts and weathered two unsuccessful marriages. Two years after joining a New York real estate agency as a secretary in 1962, the tough Brooklyn broad became a broker. Within a few years she became one of New York's few self-made millionairesses by taking advantage of conversions of apartment buildings to condominiums. In 1970 the ambitious businesswoman met Harry Helmsley, a New York real estate magnate who was once one of America's richest men. The couple married two years later, after Harry left his wife Eve with a reputed $7 million settlement and Leona promised to lose 20lbs.

They quickly joined the New York social life and proceeded to buy a Manhattan penthouse as well as a twenty-eight-room Connecticut estate, a Palm Beach condominium and a private jet. But since Leona's conviction, the society friends they once catered to have deserted them.

Leona began to gain her reputation as a monster of an employer when she decided to go back to work in 1980 and became president of the Helmsley twenty-six-hotel empire. Although her advertising campaign depicting her as a meticulous boss proved effective, her employees did not appreciate her dictatorial managing style. The hotel's motto was: "The only Palace in the world where the Queen stands guard." But this queen was not a kindly one. She fired one waiter for having dirty fingernails and another for having a trembling hand when he served her. When an unpaid contractor complained that he needed to feed his six children, Leona answered: "Why doesn't he keep his pants on, he wouldn't have so many problems." While giving a writer an interview, Leona came across a wrinkled bedspread and tilted lampshade and started screaming: "The maid's a slob! Get her out of here. Out! Out!" But despite this reputation as an insufferable employer, the stars booked in, including Frank Sinatra and arms dealer Adnan Kashoggi. Leona, worried about looking aged, enhanced her publicity photos with a computer to take decades off her face and inches off her figure.

She began to have delusions of grandeur – some likened Leona during this period to Marie Antoinette – and took up swimming in her penthouse pool as exercise. A liveried servant held a silver platter of cocktail shrimps at one end of the pool and as Leona completed each lap she would clap her hands and say: "Feed the fishy." Whereby the servant would reach down and feed her a shrimp. Unfortunately for Helmsley, her new digs will not include a pool nor a servant.

# Howard Hughes

Howard Hughes did not die in poverty, but he did lose several fortunes in his lifetime as a result of his eccentric

Pools have been running in Britain for many years, and for all who have realized their dreams and won millions, there are many "winners" like Vivian Nicholson, who frittered the money away in record time. Nicholson's husband Keith won £152,319 in the pools in 1961 – a huge sum then. His wife went wild and blew the winnings on clothes, parties, booze and race horses. When her husband died in a car crash, what little money was left disappeared. She eventually went through three husbands, a few cruises and a pink Mercedes. Nicholson later wrote a book on her experiences titled "*Spend, Spend, Spend*", which was adapted into a television play and later into a low-budget musical. She now lives in a council flat in Leeds.

ways. At nineteen he turned his share of an oil drill company into a huge fortune that included aviation, film, and gambling businesses. In the early 1950s, Hughes became a hermit and began to go inexorably mad. He was overcome by fears and phobias which his entourage indulged. They gave him everything he asked for, but not the one thing he really needed – psychiatric help. Hughes went into seclusion in Las Vegas where he became obsessed with germs, and even walked around with his feet in tissue boxes to keep them away. He was also obsessed with his own publicity and became a shy recluse who died of malnutrition in 1976 at the age of seventy in a chartered Lear jet. He reportedly hadn't cut his hair or nails for over ten years, and he died leaving $1.5 billion, and no will.

Hughes' life was a paradox: he meticulously designed airplanes and organized his flights which broke world records, yet he was a failure at manufacturing aircraft. He wrote a meticulous will at the age of nineteen before he married his first wife, Lilla Rice, yet he died without one. He was thought of as a generous man and a great benefactor, yet the Howard Hughes Medical Institute was a sham and was used by his companies for liquidity purposes. Known as a film-maker, Hughes didn't make a film for years. Once the richest man in the United States, he lost $367,579 per day for years; in all he lost about one billion dollars.

During the last twenty years or so of his life, Hughes had become a prisoner of his obsessions. He was tortured with drugs and his body became a human reservoir of codeine and valium by the time of his death. He had a tumour in his head, shrunken kidneys, and broken hypodermic needles littered his body. The billionaire who broke records for building the largest wooden plane ever to fly, lived in isolation where he reportedly consumed the greatest amount of Kleenex Tissue in history. He watched films obsessively and on a whim bought a local TV station in Las Vegas so that he could order it to run movies throughout the night. Hughes was a TV addict who watched six films at a sitting, propped up on a bed of paper tissues.

At nineteen Hughes took over the Hughes Tool Company from his father, who had invented a drill that launched the company and the family fortune. The young Hughes immediately left for Hollywood and began producing movies. He directed his first film, "Hell's Angels", starring Jean Harlow, when his director walked out on him. He ended up making the most expensive film ever made at the time, using more than eighty aircraft, flew some himself, and consequently became obsessed with film-making. The film lost millions but Hughes became a legend. After the film, Hughes became obsessed with flying and acquired the best planes he could find, altered them, and broke dozens of speed records.

Finally, he made a record-breaking round-the-world flight which lasted three days and nineteen hours and received a hero's welcome in New York upon his return.

Hughes fostered his mania for flying by starting the Hughes Aircraft Company, buying Trans World Airlines (TWA), and helping design the Lockheed Constellation – which later became one of the world's most important airliners. On 8 July 1946, Hughes nearly died when a plane he was test-flying crashed, leaving him with ten broken bones, a collapsed lung, and third-degree burns. He had been flying the XF-H reconnaissance plane he had designed himself.

As a businessman Hughes was a failure: he was chronically indecisive and often bought on a whim. The only companies he owned which did well were those which he didn't interfere with. One thing Hughes did know how to do well, however, was give handouts to everyone, from city officials to members of the Cabinet. By the 1950s he was giving out $1 million a year to "buy" people. Said Noah Dietrich, a former aide to the billionaire: "Howard had three principles: one, anyone can be bought, so find out the price; two, use other people's money; three, any trouble, fire the sonofabitch." He expected

---

**British TV star Ted Rogers, who formerly hosted a popular game show called 3–2–1, has lost his £1 million fortune. Rogers wept with shame as he told a British tabloid how a disastrous business venture left him "stony broke". He said he also cried when his showbiz friends offered to bail him out. Since surviving his debt ordeal in 1992, Rogers has lost his house, his Mercedes, and his earning power. The comedian once regularly played polo with Prince Charles and was a friend of ex-Prime Minister Margaret Thatcher. He quit his hit show in 1988 when he decided to form his own TV production company, WRTV, with two friends. By the time the recession hit, Rogers was penniless and the business was a failure.**

his bribes to buy whatever he wanted from people, including a continuation of the Vietnam War. Hughes once even tried to pay off a US president to stop testing nuclear weapons in the Nevada desert because he was afraid the noise would scare off customers from his Las Vegas hotels. He even allegedly had ties to the Watergate scandal and was instrumental in helping get President Richard Nixon into office.

The relationship between Nixon and Hughes apparently began when the billionaire was under Congressional investigation for failure to deliver on 600 planes he had promised the US government during World War II. Hughes had received $100 million in order to produce at least 500 huge plywood airplanes which would weigh 200 tons, be larger than a 747 Jumbo, and ship masses of men and material to England to help with the war effort. He was also commissioned to build and deliver 100 FX-11 airplanes, a reconnaissance bomber he nearly died in when he crashed during a test flight. The US government received only two useless prototypes for their money. They wanted to know what had happened and were planning a full-scale Congressional inquiry. When Hughes realized what was happening, he began looking for allies and found out about an ambitious young lawyer named Richard Nixon who was planning on running for Congress against a liberal Congressman in Southern California, where several of Hughes factories were located. Hughes and several other millionaire businessmen backed their candidate, who won after running a hostile anti-communist campaign. Nixon subsequently was present when Hughes faced the Congressmen at the hearing in the summer of 1947. The inquiry was dropped when key witnesses failed to appear and public opinion turned in favour of Hughes.

But the Nixon-Hughes connection didn't end there, although no one really knows how much money changed hands and how often. While running as Eisenhower's running mate during the 1952 presidential elections, Nixon was accused of giving out political favours in return for being a beneficiary of a secret millionaire's club. He successfully rebutted the accusations, however, and was elected, gathering power while Ike was away. He headed the President's committee on Government contracts, from which Hughes benefited during the Korean War when Hughes Aircraft was used. The war brought huge profits to the company, which had become a national leader in supplying missiles and sophisticated electronic weaponry.

The profits, however, were multiplied by Hughes' clever tax-evasion schemes cooked up by his advisors: they invented a medical foundation to receive surplus cash, with Hughes as the sole trustee. In 1954 the Hughes Medical Institute became the technical owner of Hughes Aircraft, pulling in millions of dollars each year. When the Internal Revenue Service refused to grant the Institute tax exemption status, Hughes once again turned to his old friend, Nixon, in return supplying him with $100,000 to fight off a Republican rival who wanted his job. He then loaned Nixon $205,000 so he could help his brother's failing "Nixon-burger" business in California. Hughes never got his money back from the Vice President, but he was granted full tax exemption for his Medical Institute one month later. Over the next twenty years, Hughes was free from paying the US Treasury an estimated $800 million in taxes.

But this wasn't enough to satisfy the billionaire who once told his closest advisor that his three goals in life were to be the world's leading aviator, its richest man, and its greatest film-maker. He strove to realize the latter achievement by filming the definitive Western to be called "The Outlaw", based on Billy the Kid's life. Hughes discovered Jane Russell – his new star – while at the dentist having his tooth filled. She was a well-endowed dental assistant who caught his eye. When Hughes began lecturing director Howard Hawkes on how the film should be shot (with an emphasis on Ms Russell's chest), the director quit and the billionaire found himself in charge. During filming Hughes specially designed a bra for his star using his aerodynamic know-how. The film, which had a budget of $3.5 million, was a flop, but the publicity surrounding the advertising campaign – the posters read, "What are the two big reasons for Jane's success?" – helped the movie do well at the box office. Hughes was also interested in Hollywood's stars and dated a host of them, including Gina Lollabridgida, Yvonne de Carlos, Jean Peters, Ava Gardner and Mitzi Gaynor. He would often promise young actresses stardom to win them over, pay-off their husbands, then dump them when he tired of them. He later bought RKO studios and lost $18 million in three

years, producing only nine pictures a year. In the 1950s
he closed the studio after claiming it was overrun with
Communists.

His breakdown seems to have occurred when he lost a
public fight to hold control of TWA in 1966. His response
to this setback was to become a recluse, and move to Las
Vegas, where he spent the half-billion dollars from the
sale of the airline on buying up property and casinos in
this gambling town. Hughes went into partnership with
the Mafia bosses there, and put the general operations of
his holdings into the hands of former FBI agent Robert
Aime Maheu, who had helped plan the CIA-backed Bay
of Pigs disaster. The billionaire set up in the ninth floor
penthouse of the Desert Inn. Already beginning to experience phobias and obsessions, he had the windows of the
apartment blacked out because he thought he had a rare
skin disease which suffered from too much light. A crew
of silent Mormons were hired to serve as his nurses, sec-
retaries, cooks, and messengers, and were separated from
him by a glass wall. He began noting intricate details to his
staff about how a car should be parked and a can should
be opened, and rarely saw his second wife, actress Jean
Peters.

Within two years of living in Las Vegas, Hughes' side-kick
had bought up six casino-hotels, an airport, two airlines,
real estate, various mining claims, and several local politi-
cians for $300 million. Meanwhile, Maheu was on call for
his boss between 12-18 hours a day. The millionaire sent
his aide to Nixon, who was then running for President
in 1968, to express his support. After giving generously
to his campaign, Nixon allegedly asked for a more "personal" contribution and Hughes sent him a secret cheque
for $100,000. In return, the captain of industry wanted
the White House to continue the war in Vietnam so that
Hughes Aircraft's military contracts would be extended.
Hughes sent Maheu a memo in 1969, telling him: "Get
to our new friends in Washington and see what can be
done to keep the war going." Next Hughes' attention was
directed towards the nuclear testing in the Nevada desert,
which he feared would deter customers from his casinos
and hotels in Las Vegas. He allegedly sent Maheu to offer
President Lyndon B. Johnson an offer of $1 million if he
would ban testing in Nevada. When Nixon took office,

Hughes also tried to persuade him to stop the testing with a $1 million bribe. Although Maheu says he never went through with the offer, the bombing stopped a few months later.

By this time Hughes' health was deteriorating: he would go fifty-two hours without sleep or food, and would only eat sweets, cakes, and cookies. When he recovered slightly, he became involved in a deal with the CIA, whereby his companies would aid them in a $350 million plan to steal secrets for a Soviet submarine that had sunk off the coast of the Bahamas. The plan, which included Hughes purchasing Paradise Island, was foiled by black nationalists on the island.

Meanwhile, Hughes made the mistake of making an enemy out of Maheu, who knew everything that had gone on between his employer and President Nixon. The *New York Times* reported in February 1972 that Maheu had deposited incriminating information about Hughes for safekeeping with Hank Greenspun, a politican who had also worked for the Hughes camp and was now head of the Democratic Party campaign. A few weeks later, Nixons "plumbers" broke into his Watergate office in Washington, and were caught attempting to steal some important papers. Their arrest led to the scandal which culminated in Nixon's resignation and ended his career.

Hughes, who was hiding out from IRS officials at the time by moving around continuously from one hotel to another, was hardly affected by the scandal. He was still lucid enough in 1973, after living in seclusion for sixteen years, to debunk an attempt to forge his memoirs and take a test flight of a 748 plane at an English airport while stark naked. Later that year, he fell while staying at the Inn on the Park in London and broke his hip. A secret operation failed to set him walking again, and from the age of sixty-eight he was bedridden. He was also suffering at this time from undiagnosed kidney problems. When a doctor was finally able to take some blood samples from Hughes when he slipped into a coma, it was too late. He died alone, a skeleton of a man wracked by paranoia and phobias, in an airplane 3,000 feet up. He weighed barely 90lbs and his body had shrunk three inches.

After his death it was discovered that he had a cousin,

> Rock star Mick Fleetwood, leader of the highly successful pop group Fleetwood Mac, blew his fortune on houses, expensive toys, women and cars. He filed for bankruptcy in 1984 with debts of more than $3.7 million. Fleetwood had to give up his houses, his cars, much of his musical equipment and his huge toy collection. His lawyer told *Rolling Stone* magazine that his client was a lover of great drums, cars, beautiful women and magnificent pieces of real estate. It was his passion for buying property, however, that put Fleetwood in the red. His problems began when he purchased some real estate in Australia in 1980. But after living there for three weeks, the rock star decided that life "Down Under" was not for him, and sold the house, taking a great loss. Unfortunately he had used his house in Beverly Hills as collateral for the purchase. The next year he bought a house in Malibu he called the "Blue Whale". He took out a second mortgage on his home, but was paying $20,000 a month in payments due to soaring interest rates. Eventually his small empire started to crumble; his investments failed and his annual earnings dropped to a third of what they had been (over $1 million a year). And Fleetwood was left with almost nothing.

William R. Lummis, who subsequently took over the crumbling Hughes empire and put the businesses into the black.

# William Randolph Hearst

The great newspaper magnate William Randolph Hearst was a millionaire for most of his life until, at the age of seventy-five and mired in the depression of the 1930s, he went bankrupt. But by the time World War II arrived, his fortune had been restored and when he died in 1951 at the age of eighty-eight, he left behind a legacy of tens of millions of dollars. He is remembered as one of the most influential American newspaper proprietors who helped mould the world's Press and created the phenomenon of yellow journalism.

The son of a millionaire, Hearst amassed two fortunes and

at the height of his success owned forty newspapers and magazines, international news, feature and film services, and controlled several radio stations. He was born in San Francisco in 1863 to Phoebe and George Hearst, who had escaped extreme poverty to become a multi-millionaire and a US Senator for California. The couple doted on their only child. When William Randolph Hearst left Harvard University at the age of twenty-two without a degree, his father acquiesced to his request for the San Francisco Examiner, which he had been losing money on for years. To begin with, his son lost a fortune on the paper. But he managed to turn it around several years later, making it self-supporting and highly successful, when it began covering crimes and scandals and made personalities its speciality. After convincing his mother to give him a large portion of the fortune his father left her (George Hearst left nothing to his son when he died), William Randolph migrated to New York and purchased a second-rate sheet he named the *New York Journal* for £36,000. He spent a fortune luring the best known journalists away from the city's other newspapers.

The *Journal* appealed to the less literate masses and Hearst became known for championing the plight of the poor. Though hated by intellectuals, Hearst was neither stupid nor stingy, but rather a highly intelligent and energetic man who was frequently generous and a patron of public causes. He was criticized for spreading what was known as "yellow journalism" across the country. The term was coined by a cartoon strip he had purchased, and did not mean merely sensational journalism, but outright lies. His newspapers deliberately falsified the news – and some of the stories he and his journalists made up were so shocking that congressional investigations were held – and advocated the practice of public character assassination. Hearst was a tyrant as an employer whose demands were never disputed, but was considered generous in dealing with his editors and managers. He knew every aspect of the newspaper business, including the mechanical side and could master any new machinery without effort. He had a good sense of popular newspaper technique and was considered an excellent newspaper writer. Hearst also had a good publicity sense: "Putting out a newspaper without promotion is like winking at a girl in the dark – well-intentioned but ineffective," said the magnate.

Soon, Hearst spread his influence to daily papers in Boston, Chicago, Los Angeles, Pittsburgh, Detroit, Baltimore, Atlanta, Omaha, and elsewhere, eventually becoming the largest newspaper proprietor in the United States. He also published a New York daily in German and sold features to a syndicate of over 2,000 American newspapers. A powerful newspaper politician, Hearst was an ineffectual political politician who failed in his bid for Governor of New York State and never realized his dream of becoming president of the United States. After overcoming his early fear of speaking in public, he was elected as a Congressman, a job at which he proved rather incompetent. Still, his experience in politics helped him to develop a talent for blunt, fervid speeches, though he sometimes declared himself a Democrat, and other times a Republican. At the turn of the century he was considered one of America's leading liberals. He later used his considerable influence as a publisher to help bring about the Spanish-American War as a way to publicize his newspapers and himself. He sent a young correspondent, Frederick Remington, to Havana to cover "the war". Remington telegraphed to his boss: "There is no trouble here. There will be no war. I wish to return." Hearst answered: "You furnish the pictures and I'll furnish the war." He later went to Cuba to report on the war himself.

With no stock-holders or lenders to influence him, he had total power over what was written in his papers. He often used his publications to serve his beliefs and principles, and tried to stop the US from entering both World Wars. Though he was branded a traitor and unpatriotic and lost millions in revenue and thousands of readers, Hearst refused to back down. Though he gained the reputation for being a fascist when he would not support fighting in World War II, he was far from that and told Hitler during their one meeting that he was out of luck as long as he persisted in his anti-Semitism.

Hearst newspapers were highly successful until after World War I when fierce competition from the tabloids began to eat into his circulation. In 1937 the *New York American* stopped publication after losing £200,000 the previous year. Hearst began to sell off his treasures in order to save his businesses. His holdings included an estate he built near San Francisco he named Wintoon – a Bavarian village which boasted timbered chalets where Hearst and his wife strolled in tyrolean hats. When he tired of that place, he went on to build San

Newspaper magnate William Randolph Hearst (centre) entertaining at his extravagant "castle" in California in the 1930s.

Simeon (Xanadu in the film Citizen Kane) on 200,000 acres in the Santa Lucia Mountains between San Francisco and Los Angeles. Hearst like to call it La Cuesta Encantada (The Enchanted Hill) or The Ranch. But the place was a palace, furnished with an array of treasures including Charles I's bed, statues, a Spanish monastery which he had shipped over in a crate and disassembled but never used because there was nowhere to fit it, three guest houses – one Moorish and two Spanish Renaissance, and a Swiss chalet wooden balcony which complemented a Gothic porch and several Mexican cupolas. One volume of the inventory of antiques in the house lists 6,776 items. Movies were shown in the private cinema. He had private railway trains built to carry his guests to San Luis Obispo, where one of his thirty-five cars would transport them to San Simeon on the six miles of private highway which crisscrossed his property. Hearst was an animal lover, and San Simeon featured a zoo and had wild animals freely roaming the grounds. Mouse-traps were banned from all his castles. Hearst Castle, as it is now known, is the most visited tourist destination in California. It took twenty-seven years and $8 million to build, and was designed by Julia Morgan, the first woman to graduate from the École des Beaux Arts in Paris as an architect. Hearst had her turn what was once a modest Spanish mission into a megalomaniac fairytale castle which they both considered a museum of architecture.

P. G. Wodehouse, who once visited Hearst at San Simeon, wrote a description of it to a friend in 1931: "The ranch – ranch, my foot; it's a castle . . . Hearst collects everything, including animals, and has a zoo on the premises, and the specimens considered reasonably harmless are allowed to roam at large. You are apt to meet a bear or two before you get to the house, or an elephant, or even Sam Goldwyn. There are always at least fifty guests staying here . . . You don't see Hearst till dinnertime . . . He's a sinister old devil, not at all the sort I'd care to meet down a lonely alley on a dark night."

Hearst had spent nearly $50 million on his collection, until he ran out of money and had to start selling pieces off. Today his treasures would be worth billions of dollars. He also sold off many of his other art treasures which were stored in five guarded warehouses in New York and used to furnish his homes there. The sale of the objects, including tapestries of four centuries, Greek sculptures, silver, furniture, armour, and paintings by Rembrandt, Hals, and Van Dyck brought in £3 million. He also sold off property he held in Wales – St Donat's Castle, which dated back to the eleventh century

---

Briton William George Stern was a tycoon with the dubious honour of holding a world record for the largest bankruptcy – he lost £104,390,248. Stern, however, was one step ahead of his creditors and had placed his house, his paintings and his Rolls-Royce under the ownership of his family trust, placing them out of their reach. The former millionaire agreed to pay £6,000 a year to settle his debts, which would leave some of his creditors waiting seventeen thousand years to be paid off.

Newspaper magnate William Randolph Hearst playing a lone game of patience in his study.

and which he had purchased in 1925 despite being fervently anti-British. He had enlarged the castle – one of seven he owned – at a great expense, while ruining old buildings elsewhere in Great Britain. Hearst also owned fruit ranches, a gold mine in Idaho and two yachts, one of which he never used.

The start of World War II – wars were good for Hearst though he was an isolationist – turned his newspaper business around again after having weathered huge deficits. Soon all of the publisher's properties were bringing in profits and Hearst was able to resume his old way of life. Though his methods of journalism were rather unsavoury, he was respected for searching out iniquities of every kind, which had a deterrent effect on corporate and individual injustices, making him a public watchdog of sorts. Yet, when he set up a newspaper business in Chicago, he employed gangsters to ruin the delivery of competing newspapers and beat up their distributers. It is said that Hearst and his competitors laid the foundation for organized crime by employing these hit men. By the time the battle had ended, twenty-seven people were dead and gangsters were established. It was also widely believed that Hearst had murdered someone on his yacht, though the allegations were never proved. When the US declared they would enter World War II in July 1940, Hearst warned that the action was a "calamity" and predicted that the winner of the war would be Russia.

Hearst had become a larger-than-life character to the American people: Orson Welles based his classic film "Citizen Kane" on the life of newspaper magnate William Randolph Hearst, who tried to buy and destroy the film. When that didn't work he tried to blackmail the cinemas not to show it (though he never saw the film), a characteristic Hearst move. Though Hearst's son, William Randolph Hearst Junior, denies that his father tried to have the film suppressed, it is known that Louis B. Meyer tried to buy Citizen Kane and dispose of it. Orson Welles was put on Hearst's black list, which consisted of 2,000 people who were banned from his newspapers, radio stations and wire services. Citizen Kane went on to win the Oscar in 1941 for best film. Welles was not the only one to portray him in film and literature; Aldous Huxley bases his eccentric treasure collector Joseph Stoyte in *After Many a Summer*" on Hearst.

The great publisher died in August 1951 at the age of

eighty-eight. He had been nursed for several years by his long-time mistress, the actress Marion Davies, who was asleep at his bedside when he died. While she slept, two of Hearst's sons carried their father's body away and when Davies awoke he was gone. His affair with Davies, a comedy actress who had starred in silent films and was forty years his junior, was said to harm Hearst's reputation in politics for leading a "loose" private life. Davies, who was faithful to Hearst until he died, became so wealthy from all his generous gifts that she was able to lend him $1 million ($25 million today) to help him recover from the Depression when his businesses fell into a slump.

Today the remainders of the original Hearst family fortune is said to be worth between $4–$5 billion. And the film based on his life which he tried so hard to have suppressed has become even more famous than him.

Eccentric billionaire James Gordon Bennett was so anxious to spend all his money that at one time he was actually found throwing thousand franc notes into the fire because they were bothering him when he sat down. In all, he managed to get through $10 million (about $280 million today). He once gave a guard on the Train Bleu between Paris and Monte Carlo a tip of $14,000 ($98,000 today). The man immediately resigned and opened a restaurant. On another occasion he bought a restaurant in Monte Carlo on the spot because someone was sitting at his favourite table. The surprised owner agreed to sell to Bennett when he was offered $40,000 ($280,000 today). The millionaire then ordered the couple to leave his table at once, and after enjoying his favourite dish (Southdown mutton chops), he gave the waiter what was probably the biggest tip he would ever receive – the restaurant.

# chapter four

# BAD LUCK

*The rise and fall of . . . Some bring it on themselves when they cannot, or will not, control their emotions, for others the bubble bursts and they find themselves out on a limb and all their friends and business associates have deserted them.*

## Bjorn Borg

At fifteen Swedish-born Bjorn Borg became the youngest player to appear in the Davis Cup. Four years later, in 1976, he launched his five-year reign as Wimbledon champion, and soon after earned the ranking of No.1 tennis player in the world. Today, however, he is a shadow of his former self. A failed comeback in 1991 showed the tennis world that he wasn't what he used to be. The path which led this former tennis phenomenon's once very promising career to take a nose-dive is littered with personal strife; divorce, corruption, an alleged suicide attempt and a failed business venture. Borg took an eight-year sabbatical from the sport before he made a failed attempt to reclaim past glories. During that period his life hit an all-time low, and the once-wealthy tennis star saw his earning power vanish.

Born in 1956 in Sodertaljie, a medium-sized town just

outside of Stockholm, Borg began playing tennis at the age of eight. The story goes that his father won a tennis racket in a table tennis competition and Borg used it to hit balls against the family garage door. He was hooked immediately. The racket was too heavy for him, however, and he developed a double-fisted backhand stroke that later became his trademark.

Three years later he came to the attention of ex-Davis Cup player Percy Rosberg, who decided to take him under his wing. "Even at the age of eleven, Borg was a dream to have on court," said Rosberg. "There were others who were prepared to spend four or five hours a day on the game – but not with the same absolute concentration. Bjorn loved tennis. Perhaps too much."

Borg soon began stacking up junior competition victories, and although many were concerned about his unconventional backhand, Rosberg decided, wisely, not to make any changes. Wimbledon veteran Lennart Bergelin took over coaching Borg when he was in his teens, becoming his travelling companion and minder as well.

At fifteen, Borg left school to become a professional tennis player and grew to rely totally on his adult protectors. He spent the next three years honing his skills and sacrificing everything else – including the life of a normal teenager. Within a short period, Borg rose to the rank of an international tennis star. He pulled in nearly fifty international singles titles, including eleven Grand Slam wins: six French Open titles and five successive Wimbledon championships. He racked up thirty-three successive single Davis Cup victories.

---

There is the story of a man from Des Moines, Iowa named Garry Llewellyn who took $15 million from his father's bank in 1982. He then took the money and blew the whole lot in Las Vegas. A few months later when the bank realized the money was missing, Llewellyn could not remember how he had spent the whole amount. He was taken to court and found insane by reason of being a compulsive gambler.

One eighteenth century gent was so addicted to gambling that he once bet a huge amount of money on which raindrop out of two would be the first to hit the windowsill at his London club. He lost.

Bjorn Borg the success story on the tennis court.

He set himself apart from his challengers by his apparently unbreakable concentration and his ability to achieve victory after victory. During this time Borg also began finding a bevy of tennis groupies wherever he went and became the first tennis sweetheart. But at the age of twenty-one, he broke many hearts when he married Romanian tennis player Marian Simionescu – who gave up her career to help him.

Soon Borg found himself an international icon as a result of all his winnings. He also became the object of criticism among the tennis circuit. Sports writers and fellow tennis players criticized Borg for being a boring player, and he was once likened to a Volvo because he was rugged, had good after-sales service and was very dull. Other critics said Borg was merely an efficient athlete rather than a brilliant one. At the height of his career, people began to describe him as inhuman because of his mechanical way of playing and winning. He was called "Ice-borg", a tennis machine. Borg, who reportedly had a resting pulse rate of 35 – half the adult norm, would only reply, "My life is tennis."

In 1981, Borg's winning streak at Wimbledon ended when John McEnroe beat him in the final. It was a devastating defeat for Borg and his fans. Later that year he lost again to McEnroe in the finals of the US Open, and Borg walked off in a huff. The next year he decided to forgo Wimbledon and the Grand Prix championships and take an experimental holiday from the game. By 1983, he had announced his retirement from tennis – to commence after the tournament in Monte Carlo. After losing there to Henri Leconte, Borg promised that nothing would ever get him back to competitive tennis. He had simply lost his motivation to play.

After leaving the sport, Borg did some promotional work for the Swedish tourist board and the Swedish airline SAS. He then decided to try his hand at business and invested some money and time into a company called Bjorn Borg Invest, which dealt mainly with real estate. He left the business decisions to others and began jet-setting around the world to revel in his freedom from tennis. But things soon began to go sour. His marriage to Simionescu broke up shortly after he left tennis when he met fellow Swede Jannaike Bjorling while judging a Miss Wet T-Shirt contest in Stockholm. In 1985, she bore him a son called Robin. But family life was not enough for Borg and he became restless again.

Borg next decided to expand his business interests to keep him occupied and in 1987 he set up the Bjorn Borg Design Company, manufacturing Borg sportswear, luggage and aftershaves called Signature and 6–0. It was a chance for Borg to do something big with his name. He made millions with the business, but made the mistake of letting others make the decisions. A year later, Borg started travelling again and split up with Bjorling when he met Loredana Berte, an Italian pop star. The former couple first shared custody of their three-year-old son, but when Borg's new relationship surfaced, Bjorling went to court to win full custody of the child. Borg also demanded the same and a lengthy court battle followed, with both participants accusing the other of being an unfit parent. Bjorling claimed Borg was a cocaine addict and he retaliated by accusing her of being promiscuous.

But Borg's new partner – whom he later married – was not the young innocent either. Berte had appeared in porn movies and magazines before reaching stardom as a pop singer. The Swedish tabloids took the couple to task –

Bjorn Borg the ill-fated businessman, launching his range of menswear at Harrods in London.

especially since she was a foreigner and fourteen years older than Borg. In 1989, Borg hit bottom and allegedly overdosed on sleeping pills. Many blamed the incident on his new wife, but others said he did it because he knew his business was going under. Shortly thereafter, the Bjorn Borg Design Company was declared bankrupt and Borg's partner Lars Skarke announced that the other Borg companies would be sold off, then turned around and sued the former tennis star for £50 million for not showing enough interest in the business and consequently wasting a potential £200 million in profits.

Borg was so desperate to get out of this mess that he offered to pay the creditors' claims (estimated at about £3 million) out of his own pocket. He then began selling off his life insurance policies and furniture to raise the money, and had his house repossessed. The court case to determine who will pay the creditors' claims, now estimated at nearly three times the original amount, still hasn't ended. Borg's lawyer, Henning Sjostrom, has counselled his client not to pay out the whole sum.

His second court case involving the custody of his son has finally been settled, however, with both parents agreeing to joint custody. Since that time – after eight years away from professional tennis, Borg has made one failed comeback attempt. Some blame the loss on his stubborn refusal to use the new high-tech graphite rackets and stick to his wooden rackets instead. He has since switched to the newer designs and now, at the age of thirty-five, is planning another try at the 1992 Monte Carlo tournament. Many assume he is doing this for the money, but it may well be a chance to find once again the fame and glory he experienced as an international tennis star.

# Mike Tyson

When he became the youngest heavyweight boxing champion at the age of twenty, Mike Tyson seemed to be embarking on an incredibly successful career and was already considered one of the world's great heavyweights of all time. But six years later, Tyson's fall was a knockout by all accounts.

On 10 February 1992, "Iron" Mike Tyson was sentenced to ten years in prison for raping and sexually assaulting a beauty contestant in Indiana. Desiree Washington was an eighteen-year-old participant in a Miss Black America pageant in Indianapolis last July when she met Tyson. He offered to take her for some late night sightseeing, but when they ended up in his hotel room instead, the pleasant evening turned into a night that would change Tyson's life forever. Washington said the fighter pinned her down and raped her, then suggested she take his limousine back to her room.

The subsequent trial turned into a predictable media circus, but despite a tough defence team, the jury of twelve convicted Tyson on one count of rape and two counts of sexually deviant conduct. And the judge handed out a stiff sentence – six years in one of the grimmest jail complexes in Indiana. Tyson, who was a multi-millionaire by the age of twenty-two, is now thought to be broke, and isn't expected to have much money left after he pays his $2 million defence bill and settles a series of outstanding actions against him. He is also expected to face a huge lawsuit from Desiree Washington, the woman he raped. A six-year prison term also means that his earning power has vanished.

When Tyson was asked how he managed to spend $40 million in two years, he said: "I don't know. Money doesn't matter. You can always get more money." While in Indianapolis during the pageant, the boxer and his associates were carrying around between $30,000 and $50,000 – in cash. According to Washington, someone approached her before the trial and offered her $1 million if she would drop the rape charge against Tyson. The Federal Bureau of Investigation is looking into who made the offer.

If Tyson were still fighting today, he might have become the greatest and richest heavyweight of all time. During his five-year reign, he earned about $100 million. His fight with Michael Spinks brought him $21 million – or $145,000 per second (Tyson knocked Spinks out in ninety seconds). Some boxing experts say that even with an eight-year absence, he could still achieve that honour at the age of thirty-three. Seth Abraham, head of Time-Warner Sports, said Tyson's departure will have "the most profound effect on the heavyweight championship, and that connects with the other divisions. As the heavyweight division goes, so goes boxing." Others say that Tyson's departure from boxing was actually good for the sport because it meant the elimination of someone who is perceived to be a bad apple.

Psychiatrists say it is precisely that aspect of Tyson's personality, his naked aggression and pure animal brutality, that brought the crowds in to see him. They wanted to see "the baddest man on the planet." But those who worked with him said he neglected the basics in training when he began to believe what people were writing and saying about him – that he was invincible.

Tyson's career as a boxer began when he was plucked out of a juvenile detention hall in upstate New York by legendary fight trainer and manager Cus D'Amato when he was thirteen-years-old. This was the beginning of his rags-to-riches dream. D'Amato set Tyson up in his three-storey, seven bedroom house in the Catskill region of New York, a far cry from the boy's upbringing in the mean streets of Brooklyn where violence was part of his repertoire of survival skills. Soon after the trainer legally adopted the young fighter and set to work over the next nine years on making his dream come true by turning Tyson into a prizefighter before he died. But D'Amato didn't regard Tyson as a son, merely as an investment into the glory of training another heavyweight champion. He trained Tyson by honing his instincts for violence to a fine edge, cultivating all those qualities in the fighter that society condemns. By the time he was fifteen, he had left school, was being educated by a tutor, and was basically a full-time professional fighter. Although Iron Mike wasn't smooth and quick on his feet like Muhammed Ali or Sugar Ray Leonard, he was menacing and would smash his opponents mercilessly. One victim described being hit by Tyson: "My neck went down into my belly-button." His rage produced a sense of awe in his observers and terrified his opponents. Former world champion Michael Spinks was so intimidated by the prospect of fighting Tyson that he was said to have simply dissolved in front of him; another opponent, Alex Stewart, passed out after two minutes of fighting the champion – but more of fainting from fright than from the force of Tyson's blows. Statements Tyson made about his opponents, such as "I tried to drive the bone of his nose back into his brain", added to his image of being incredibly violent and merciless.

Other comments Tyson made regarding his boxing tech-nique to former boxer Jose Torres for his book *Fire and Fear* made people wonder if Iron Mike was human at all. "I feel so good when you're in pain. I'm always thinking about taking an icepick and sticking it in somebody's ear or stabbing somebody in the eye, just biting them or ripping their lips off," he said, explaining that it was fear that made him so violent. But it wasn't just the fear of getting hurt that motivated Tyson, it was the fear of being ridiculed.

The one person who humiliated him publicly and got away with it, was his former wife, actress Robin Givens. On a prime-time national television talk show, she analyzed and ridiculed Tyson while he just sat there silently watching. Many say that when Givens realized that they had no future together, she was determined to take her cut from Tyson's fortunes. She tried to cash a check for $500,000 from their joint account before Tyson's new boxing manager Don King found out about the suit and told him to close the account. King took over as Tyson's manager when Cus D'Amato died in 1985, three years before Tyson became the youngest world heavyweight champion in history. He never lived to see his dream realized. King, a well-known boxing promoter, took this as an opportunity to take advantage of the distraught Tyson, and signed him to a four-year exclusive promotional contract which held the boxer to punitive clauses that gave him no control over whom, when and where he fought.

Although King didn't take to Givens and mistrusted her, some members of Tyson's camp say she was good for the boxer. He didn't even have his own bank account before she arrived and when he wanted to buy a new car, he had to ask his managers if he could have some money. But even King's power couldn't stop the jury from convicting Tyson for his crime, nor from sending him to jail. He has since retained high-profile defence lawyer and Harvard professor Alan Dershowitz to defend him in an appeal of his rape conviction. The champion's life has come full circle and he has ended up where he started – behind bars.

Since starting his new life in jail, Tyson has already run into trouble. He was placed in solitary confinement after threatening to "whup" a prison guard, was disciplined for giving his autograph to inmates, and was reprimanded after allegedly having sex with a girlfriend during a visiting session. He reportedly told friends that he wants a reconciliation with his ex-wife Robin Givens.

# Ronald Biggs

Ronald "Biggsie" Biggs was a small-time thief who became a folk hero in Britain after he successfully robbed £2.5 million from a train, and escaped from the British justice system by fleeing to South America. He lived happily in Brazil for

Henry Ford was a mechanical genius who invented the Model-T and made the automobile affordable to the average man through his use of mass production. He built himself a huge industrial empire and an immense fortune, which he came close to losing several times in his career. Ford was a visionary who was concerned about ordinary people and introduced new concepts for higher wages, shorter working hours, and better methods of salesmanship. He was willing to employ anyone who would do the job right – including former prisoners. In 1893, Ford invented the first "gasoline buggy" using a silent gas engine and at its first public trial it reached a speed of twenty-five miles per hour. After building some highly successful race cars, Ford was able to raise enough money through the publicity to start his own company building cars, and in 1903 the Ford Motor Company was born. He founded the business with a capital of $100,000 and was soon a success. In 1908 he built his famous "Model-T" and eventually devised the idea of the assembly line. Though he later built the Eagle submarine chasers for the war effort, Ford was a pacifist and refused to profit from the war. In 1920, his company faced a serious financial situation, but he eventually found a way out of it. In 1931 his 20,000,000th car came off the assembly line, but it was during the depression and that same year his company lost nearly $20 million. World War II saved Ford's company and his company and fortunes were revived. Ford, however, died a defeated man after his company lost a long-standing battle with the unions for more power and the Ford Motor Company was closed to union members only.

several years before he was discovered there. Fortunately for him, under Brazilian law the father of a Brazilian child could not be extradited and Biggs had just fathered a child he named Mike. But Biggs, who has already spent most of the money he stole by trying to fight extradition to Britain, may have found that his luck has finally run out. His son is about to turn eighteen, and Biggs's protected status as the father of a Brazilian child, which has kept him from being returned to jail thus far, is about to run out. The great escaper had eluded the law for nearly thirty years. "So many Britons who come to Rio seek me out just to shake my hand and get my autograph. They treat me as a hero because I beat the rap. The Brazilians welcome me wherever I go, too," Biggs has said.

Biggs was a decorator who had done some petty crime in the past but had been straight for three years, when in 1963 he was asked at the last minute to join a band of thieves who planned on robbing a mail train in the remote English countryside as it made its way to London from Scotland. "I asked for twenty-four hours to think it over." I suppose I needed about twenty seconds. "Put my name on the list," I said, "I can get you a train driver," Biggs said in a recent interview. The robbers knew that attached to the train would be a special coach carrying banknotes arranged to be destroyed in London. They believed that on this journey the booty could be as much as £4 million. The group consisted of Bruce Reynolds, thirty, who wanted to live a life of luxury; Gordon Goody, thirty-two, a loner who liked fine clothes and women; Ronald "Buster" Edwards, thirty, a club-owner; Charlie Wilson, thirty-two; Jimmy White, forty-two, an ex-paratrooper; Bob Welch, thirty-two, a London club owner; Tommy Wisbey, thirty-two, a bookmaker; and Jim Hussey, a thirty-year-old Soho restaurateur. The specialists of the bunch were: Roy James, twenty-three, a silversmith and racing driver who did the driving; Roger Cordrey, thirty-eight, a florist with an expertise at fixing railway signalling equipment; and a retired train driver. They chose a bridge in a quiet spot in Buckinghamshire to do their deed, and waited for the train at a farmhouse twenty-six miles from the site.

At midnight, dressed in commando gear, they headed for their destiny in two Land Rovers and a lorry and prepared for the train's arrival by cutting all emergency telephone lines. When the train arrived at 3 a.m., it slowed down then stopped when the driver saw a red signal light overhead. The plan was immediately set in motion after the train's fireman was knocked out while going to check the problem. Everything went according to their scheme, until the train driver, Jack Mills, was hit twice on the head. This later proved to be a fatal mistake for the robbers, who would have got off easier at their trial if the driver hadn't been seriously injured. Mills never fully recovered from his injuries and died of leukaemia seven years later. Biggs and the old railwayman had waited in one of the Land Rovers while the plan was carried out, and when the former driver was unable to start the train, the injured Mills was forced to sit at the controls, with a trickle of blood running down his forehead. Meanwhile, the five Post Office guards were made to lie down on the floor while the group unloaded the 120 mailbags and transferred them to their lorry by way of a human chain. They immediately drove back to the farmhouse, where they spent the night counting out the money they had stolen – £2.5 million.

Although they had all arranged alibis and planned not to spend the money for some time, their strategy was bungled when evidence they had left behind – fingerprints, clothing and vehicles – was discovered by police. The men were identified by their finger and palm prints, and most were in jail within a year. Biggs escaped with his share – £140,000 – until he was caught. Goody, Welch, James, Wisbey, Hussey, Wilson and Biggs were all sentenced to thirty years in prison. All but Wilson and Biggs were out of jail in twelve years; Cordrey was freed after serving seven years of a fourteen year term. White fled and eluded police for three years until he was caught. He ended up serving nine years in jail. Reynolds and Edwards hid out for a while, then escaped to Mexico City for three years until they ran out of money and returned to Britain. They were arrested soon after and spent their time in jail as well.

The Great Train Robbers soon became the Great Escapers when Wilson escaped from a Birmingham prison in 1965 and fled to Mexico City. He was arrested after he moved to Montreal and was caught there, and returned to England to spend ten more years in prison. But Biggs's escape was the most extraordinary – some friends helped spring him from jail after he scaled the prison walls and jumped onto the roof of a waiting van. He fled to France, where for £40,000 he underwent plastic surgery to alter his looks and was given a new identity and a one-way ticket to wherever he wanted to

Great Train Robber Ronald Biggs leaving a courtroom in Barbados.

Ronald Biggs hugs his lawyers in Barbados.

go. He chose Australia, where he lived with his wife and three sons as Terence Furminger for several years. When he found out that Scotland Yard was on to him, he escaped again – this time to Brazil – on the passport of an old friend named Mickey Haynes. He later named his son after this man. Biggs set up a new life there in Rio de Janeiro, and turned to drugs, alcohol and women to fill the empty void in his life. Then, in 1974, a London newspaper reporter tracked him down with plans to write his story. Scotland Yard was tipped off and attempted to arrest Biggs and take him back to England, when they found out that Brazil did not have an extradition agreement with Britain. He then received another stroke of luck, when his Brazilian girlfriend, Raimunda, announced that she was pregnant with his child – fathers of Brazilian children could not be deported.

Biggs lived peacefully in Rio de Janeiro and says he came closest to giving himself up when one of his sons was killed in an automobile accident in Australia. In 1981, his tranquil life in Brazil was shattered when a gang of kidnappers led by a former British Army sergeant named John Miller abducted him and smuggled him out of the country. They deposited their prize aboard a private yacht and sailed to Barbados where they held Biggs ransom and attempted to sell him to the highest bidder. But when their yacht was seized by the Coastguard, the kidnappers fled and their victim was thrown into an island jail to await deportation to Britain. Fortunately, the law was on his side once again and after some friends in Brazil hired a top lawyer to fight for him, the island judge declared that Biggs could not be extradited to England. The legal fees cost him £30,000 – but he was free again.

The Great Escaper still lives in Rio de Janeiro with his son Mike, who was a child pop star for a while in a band called The Magic Balloon Gang, and spends time with his long-term Argentinian girlfriend, Ulla. Biggs is barred from working by the Brazilian government but makes his living by being a celebrity: making TV commercials, selling T-shirts emblazoned with his name, doing interviews, and advising pop groups. When asked if he regrets his crime, Biggs said in a recent interview: "We all reflect on things and arrive at this word 'regret'. I don't think you could say my life has turned out all right. I lost my wife and my children when I disappeared to Rio and five years later my protected status as Mike's father did not extend to them." Biggs says the reason his freedom was so important was so that his children wouldn't have to bear the stigma of having a father in prison.

# Willie Nelson

Country and Western singer Willie Nelson has found a new partner in his latest musical endeavour: the US Internal Revenue Service. The musician must sell four million copies of his latest album, Who'll Buy My Memories, in order to pay off his tax debts of $32 million. Nelson, fifty-eight, was allowed to enter his recording studio, which the IRS had sealed after seizing and auctioning all of his assets in 1990, so he could compile an album out of the thirty-five years of private recordings he kept. The only possession he was allowed to keep was his old Martin guitar. "I have been broke

Film director Peter Bogdanovich filed for bankruptcy in 1985 with nothing left of his $6 million fortune except for his house and $47.16. The director of such films as The Last Picture Show and Paper Moon, Bogdanovich tragically spent the money trying to immortalize Dorothy Stratten, the woman he loved. A former Playmate of the Year for *Playboy* magazine, Stratten was starring in a film he was directing called "They All Laughed". The couple fell in love during filming and were planning to marry. Stratten's estranged husband put an end to their bliss, however, when he murdered her and then killed himself. Bogdanovich was heartbroken and spent $5 million to buy the rights of the film and distribute it as a memorial to her. But the movie bombed and he was left with $6.6 million in debts.

before and I'll be broke again. Heartbroke? That's serious. Lose a few bucks? That's not," said Nelson. The profits from his new album, which was first sold by telephone for $19.95 (£11.80), will be divided up, with half going to the telemarketing company selling the recording, $2.40 going to the Sony Corporation, $1.40 for production costs. Nelson's profits – $6 per album – will be divided between the IRS to pay for back taxes and taxes on the recording, and for the musician's suit against his accountants, Price Waterhouse, whom he says wrongly advised him on how to invest his money.

This is the second in Nelson's spate of recent bad luck. In December 1991, the country star's son committed suicide at his Nashville home on Christmas Day. His friends said he had alcohol and employment problems and felt he hadn't measured up to his father's expectations.

Friends of the singer, have set up a "Willie Fund" in order to help bail him out. Nelson's road to success was a rocky one. He was born into relative poverty in Texas where he was a starving songwriter until his songs were discovered by Nashville's country and western stars in the early Sixties and he was inducted into the Grand Ole Opry. Hundreds of artists were recording his songs, but his own record sales were dreadful. He failed to capitalize on his early fame and became a frustrated musician who couldn't convince people to recognize him as a singer in his own right. Record executives and booking agents in Nashville wouldn't accept the changes Nelson wanted to make in his music, which was influenced by pop, jazz and blues. He turned to hard liquor and drugs to ease his pain, ended up with two broken marriages, and in the mid-1960s went into semi-retirement. In 1969, after his second divorce and with his career at a standstill, Nelson recorded a song with Hank Cochran called "What Can You Do to Me Now?" The next day, his house burned down.

It wasn't until he decided to try a new, more radical brand of country in the Seventies after returning to his home in Texas that he found real success. The singer bought a used Greyhound bus and started giving concerts locally, building up a redneck, long-haired following. When Nelson realized that young rock fans were also interested in country music, he began playing to this new audience by growing a beard, letting his red hair grow long and wearing it in braids, and tying a bandanna around his head. He also sported an earring stud. This became his trademark look and his new fans loved it – he had legitimized country music for the under-thirties. His real breakthrough came when he moved to Columbia Records from Atlantic Records and was given creative control for the first time. His first album for them, "Red Headed Stranger", was a concept recording which included old country standards and Nelson originals and was a huge success. He then formed the Outlaws with Waylon Jennings, Tompall Glaser and Jessi Colter.

Nelson soon became both a country and pop hit and broadened his appeal with a gospel album, a Christmas collection and tribute albums to other songwriters. After his most successful mainstream pop album, "Stardust", Nelson's popularity hit an all time high and he started performing in Las Vegas showrooms and helped market Willie Jeans. In 1980 his records sold about five million copies and he starred in a hit film, "Honeysuckle Rose", with Amy Irving. While not working, Nelson was dividing his time between his homes and ranches in Texas, Colorado, Tennessee and California. He used to own a Lear Jet, but sold it because he thought it was too extravagant.

In 1990, he formed and toured with The Highwaymen, comprised of Waylon Jennings, Kris Kristofferson, and Johnny Cash, as well as touring with his own group, The Family Band. He also starred in The Electric Horseman with Robert

Redford and Barbarosa with Gary Busey, and wrote his autobiography titled simply *"Willie"*.

Nelson is a staunch Democrat who endorsed Jesse Jackson in 1987 and is friends with Jimmy Carter. He was asked to run for Senate in Texas, but declined. "I'm an entertainer. Why should I cut off half my audience and say screw you? That'd be a horrible thing to do to your career. I sit on the sidelines and make suggestions," said the singer, who tells in his autobiography how he once smoked a joint on the roof of the White House.

He has a general store, a pool hall, and a road named in his honour, as well as a song by jazz great Miles Davis who wasn't known to be fond of country musicians. Despite all the honours and the record sales, two of his forty-eight albums – Stardust and Always on my Mind – sold three million copies each, Nelson is now hoping his latest album will sell enough to pay off the taxman.

# Buster Keaton

Regarded as one of the great comedians of all time, Buster Keaton was at the forefront of moving pictures in the 1920s, but his success as a silent film star and director was destroyed by the businessmen who moved into Hollywood and changed it into a homogenous world where talented individuals had no part. He had been a successful actor and director, but died in poverty a broken man.

Keaton was born in 1895 into a showbiz family: his mother was known as "America's First Woman Saxophonist" and his father was Joe ("Hitch-Kick") Keaton, a slapstick comedian who used his feet to express himself. He was able to jump four-feet into the air and kick out in the middle of the jump, and used to kick his enemies through plateglass windows in tavern brawls. Buster had been incorporated into their act ever since he had inadvertently crawled on stage at the age of nine months and got laughs. Billed as the "living mop", his father used to kick him around on stage, and the boy grew up impervious to damage, eventually turning to slapstick comedy like his father. Meanwhile, Joe Keaton was pursued by a society for the prevention of cruelty to children and criticized by Fatty Arbuckle for kicking his son during a film. "I've been kicking that boy's ass ever since he was born, and now you tell me how," said the angry father. One ad for the act read: "Maybe you think you were handled roughly when you were a kid. Watch the way they handle Buster." In states where there were strict child labour laws, Joe Keaton tried to convince them that little Buster was really a midget.

The premise of the act was Buster's stage disobedience, which was beaten into him, along with his stone-faced expression. "My father and I used to hit each other with brooms, occasioning from me strange flops and falls. If I should chance to smile, the next hit would be a good deal harder. All the parental correction I ever received (was) with

Famous singer and actress Judy Garland who played Dorothy in the Wizard of Oz, was born Frances Gumm on 10 June 1922. Her studio, MGM, would later change both her name and her birthdate (so that they could claim she was actually twelve years old at the time, rather than thirteen), and Garland would one day blame them for changing her life, too, by allegedly forcing her to become addicted to drugs. As a child performing with her sisters in their trio the Gumm Sisters, Judy could out-sing them and already had a remarkable stage presence. At the age of twelve, her voice could fill a large theatre without a microphone. When her older sister married, Judy struck out on her own and was auditioned and signed-up by MGM. Her leap to stardom came when she played Dorothy in The Wizard of Oz – though Louis B. Mayer reportedly really wanted Shirley Temple to take the part. Garland was paid $350 a week to perform in the film, and after its release she received a new contract with a substantial salary hike. Within a few years, Garland started taking pills so that she could lose weight and have more energy. During the last years of her life, she often blamed MGM for ruining her life by allegedly forcing the drugs on her. She was taking Benzedrine and Dexedrine among other drugs, and soon became erratic in her work – nearly always arriving later for a shoot or rehearsals. Eventually, her career faltered and her earning power vanished, with Garland struggling to overcome her drug addiction problem.

an audience looking on. I could not even whimper." His "frozen face" hid the hurt, terror and rage he felt. He finally found his revenge against his father by tearing up a contract to perform in a Broadway show for $240 a week and go to work making films for $40 a week.

The tumbles he took with his father enabled the young Keaton to later fall down ravines and stand sacks of flour or custard-pies being tossed at him without a hitch. He even convinced Harry Houdini to teach him how to pick locks and make "escapes". Buster had been performing in the family vaudeville act, The Four Keatons, for seventeen years, when he met Arbuckle while walking down Broadway one day on his way to rehearsals for a Broadway show. The famous comedian asked the young Keaton to come to the studio and do a scene or two with him. He went on to appear in his first film, The Butcher Boy, with Arbuckle – his performance in that movie was shot without rehearsal or retakes. After eighteen months in the Army, he came back to play his first lead in a feature film, The Saphead. He later rewarded Arbuckle for his apprenticeship by giving him thirty-five per cent of all his Keaton Production profits.

Keaton's style of concise timing, accuracy, and restraint in performing the gags was a great contrast to the rest of Arbuckle's troupe. While he worked with them, the company's pace became more constrained and refined. Soon, this comic genius with the strange solemn face, intense concentration and great eyes moved into making his own motion pictures in the early days of Hollywood when actors and directors had the freedom to be creative and do whatever they wanted. Keaton, aged twenty-one when he started, was able to make it all up as he went along, with the help of talented cameramen who invented devices at the spur of the moment that were feats of extraordinary ingenuity. He was himself a master of cinema method and from childhood he was fascinated by mechanical problems and devices. Keaton loved machines and inventing things, and tore apart a motion picture camera when he first went to work for Arbuckle so he could figure out how it worked. He grew up during a time when there was great industrial expansion in the United States, and some say his frenzied clowning was a violent response to a violent society. His later works displayed a mastery of camera and process tricks which are still unsurpassed today. His use of back projection and multiple exposure techniques were used before their time, and some of his tricks have never been completely explained. Keaton had an impeccable sense of structure: his gags fit in to the plot perfectly and were an important element of the story. Some of the great stunts included a whole wall falling on the comic – with him standing exactly in the path of its window frame with only three inches of clearance (in Steamboat Bill Jnr). The writers on the film walked off the set because the shot was so dangerous. In one stunt, the comedian jumped off a moving train, rolled down a steep embankment into a hamlet, then through the swing doors of the saloon and into the gunman who was holding up the joint. In the 1923 film The Three Ages, of which he was actor, director and editor, Keaton escapes from a police station, climbs onto a roof, springboards onto a ledge, falls three storeys through awnings and grabs onto a drainpipe which breaks and throws him through a window two floors below which is a fire station. He ends up on a fire engine which is driving off to put out a fire – at the police station from which he just escaped.

In 1920 Keaton formed his own production company and filmed Backstage (1918), One Week (1920) and the celebrated Steamboat Bill Jnr. (1928). He used trains and boats in his sets and was meticulous in his use of realistic staging. His films were made slowly and there was never a script. Said Keaton of his method: "(I would) get with a few writers, about three of them, and work until we'd got something we thought would make a story. Then we'd go ahead with the movie. There wasn't even a shooting-script. When it came to properties you'd tell the man a row of houses there, a cabin, or whatever, and he'd go off and make them. I didn't have any fixed acting company, but we had ensemble playing; if any ideas came up while we were shooting, fine, we'd use them. It was flexible."

Playhouse, considered one of the best shorts he filmed, has Keaton playing all the players in a vaudeville theatre and the audience as well. In The Boat (1921), the comedian tells the story of a man who builds a boat in the basement of his house, then finds that the boat is too big for the opening and pulls away the foundations of the house; the ship is launched, but sinks as soon as it gets into water. This sequence is reputed to have notched up one of the longest laughs in cinema history. "I had to work like a dog to get the bugs out of that scene," Keaton later explained. "First you find a wooden boat won't sink, you've got to make it sink – the whole thing has to be perforated with holes so that no air pockets collect. Then you find it won't slide down the slip-way, it has to be pulled. We fixed that with a cable and a sea-anchor. The same things came up over again when Paramount did a remake of the scene in The Buster Keaton Story, and I ironed out the bugs for them in five minutes. But that scene alone cost them $60,000 to make – making The Boat, my salary included, cost $22,000." The Saphead (1920) features a character who is a rich spoilt simpleton, who returned frequently in later films. In 1923, Keaton directed his first feature titled The Three Ages, a parody of intolerance which takes place in the Stone Age, Roman times, and the 1920s. Buster, an extraordinary athlete, performed all of his own stunts and didn't use doubles or safety nets in his films: he almost drowned making Hospitality (1923), broke his leg on The Electric House and broke his neck on Sherlock Jnr.

Over the next five years, Keaton made nine films. Though some said he was unemotional and inhuman in these, and was known as the "frozen face" or the "stone face", Keaton actually had a subtle way of showing expression: a slow blink meant a climax of joy, a hat thrown in the air is an expression of ecstasy. In truth, his face was one of the most expressive the screen has shown us. When asked why he never smiled, he replied: "I had other ways of showing I was happy". He said that he learned on the stage not to smile because he found that if he laughed at his own gags, nobody else did. So he stopped laughing. In a scene in The Cameraman, Keaton's character reacts to the girl he loves going off with another man by simply sinking to his knees. Yet, Keaton's characters always triumph in the end through their ingenuity. Small, alone and vulnerable, these characters are also self-reliant, endlessly resourceful, and indomitable. His plots usually centered around an unaided hero with a great problem who must set out to discover the solution. In The Navigator, the hero and his bride are alone on a deserted ocean liner sailing the seas, and he overcomes such problems as cooking breakfast for two in a kitchen geared to 300. Soon, Keaton's films took off and the money began pouring in. His film, The General, is set during the US Civil War and is considered the masterpiece of silent film comedy, containing meticulous period detail. When Keaton was asked why he thought his film was so much better than Gone With the Wind, he answered: "They went to a novel; I went to the history books."

Once the talkies became popular and moguls and tycoons moved into Hollywood, they made it impossible for Keaton to have the autonomy he needed to be creative. The comedian was eventually squeezed out and he never directed another film. His personal life, too, proceeded to fall apart and his first wife, Natalie Talmadge divorced him. An exceedingly passive person, Keaton would mutter, "No debates, no debates", when refusing to fight with her. When she banished him from their bed after three years of marriage and two children – Keaton did not object. He had lived as a prince in the Twenties. He earned $3,000 a week and lived in a palatial Hollywood mansion where he had six servants and gave fabulous parties. A valet dressed him and his wife ran the house.

After the divorce, his life changed dramatically – his wife even had the names of their children changed. Keaton lost the production company which he used to create his films, and made a failed attempt to make films for MGM. When that didn't work because of the restrictions imposed on the comic by the studio, he became an alcoholic and disappeared for twenty years, often broke. In one year, his income had dropped from $147,300 (in 1932) to $47,400 (in 1933). He went into a sanatorium where he woke up one day to find himself married to his nurse – echoing a film he made years before in which the character is seeking a bride, falls asleep in a church and wakes up to find himself surrounded by hundreds of women who want to be his bride.

After recovering from his alcoholism he slowly went back to work, taking bit parts in commercials and on television and making stage appearances in Europe. At the age of sixty-four, this short, stocky man had the appearance of a tough, leathery veteran and spoke with a punch, gravel-throated directness. Keaton's abilities as a performer were rediscovered when he appeared as one of a group of old-time actors gathered at a ghostly party in the film

Sunset Boulevard in 1950. A year later he appeared briefly in Limelight with Charles Chaplin, stealing the picture from him.

Keaton reassembled much of his work in 1944, along with Raymond Rohauer, a silent film enthusiast, and spent almost half his life in the struggle to re-establish himself. He died in 1966 of lung cancer, still anxious in his last few days to do some work. He had directed and starred in several talkies, which he later said he disliked, blaming MGM and their writers for the failure of the films.

The comedian later criticized the way the new films were made: "Action. That's what went out when the talkies came in. It's like vaudeville. In the old days you really had variety: variety of pianists, comics, singers. Then the thing went into a decline, and now there are no schools to train those kind of people. It's the same in movies. When talking pictures arrived the edict went around Hollywood – they all have to talk; and they overloaded the scripts with talk, unnecessary talk – it was a novelty. The script writers got an upper hand and action got left out. There'd never have been comics like Bob Hope and Benny in the pre-talkie era; the only ones who could have fitted in is Red Skelton. And Lupino Lane in England. But with somebody like me, you don't give me a long speech to recite. Let somebody else say it, let somebody else do the explaining."

His greatest films were thought to have been destroyed, until the actor James Mason discovered a secret vault in one of Keaton's former mansions which was filled with the comedian's work. The comic later became a hero to surrealists like Frederico Garcia Lorca and Louis Bunuel because of his exploration of illusion and reality. Though many consider Charlie Chaplin to be the king of silent films, Keaton is now thought of his equal, if not even more talented. In the way that Chaplin comically deflates human dignity, Keaton made comedy out of upholding human dignity in the most improbable circumstances. And though Chaplin was a great actor, Keaton was that as well as a great director. Yet, he was a modest man. Said Rohauer: "The strange thing about him is that he never understood why people found him funny. He hated making personal appearances, and would never sit in a theatre where his films were played. He was always afraid the audience wouldn't laugh." For many film experts,

> The Marx Brothers were regarded as comedians for connoisseurs and their lunacy was a relief for the masses when they first achieved success after the great Wall Street Crash of 1929. Chico Marx was the oldest; the fat, dark, curly-haired piano player with the wicked gleam in his eye. He was born into a poor immigrant family in New York with his brothers Groucho and Zeppo. The trio later formed the Marx Brothers after their ambitious mother urged them to start a vaudeville act. Their lunatic clowning on stage eclipsed their singing and after establishing a reputation nationwide, they went to Hollywood where they starred in a string of successful comedies, including "A Night at the Opera", "A Day at the Races", and "Horse Feathers". Chico played the perfect middleman to Groucho's insults and the angelic madness of Harpo, and was in fact a talented pianist who played the instrument in their act in a lightning fast manner. Along with his brothers, Chico created many original comic routines which were later extensively imitated. Chico Marx died at the age of seventy after having lost much of the fortune he made in films.

Keaton is considered the equal of any film-maker working in Hollywood today.

# Joe Louis

Joe Louis, who held the heavyweight boxing title for twelve years and was considered one of the greatest boxers of all time, died nearly penniless after the government attempted to collect on the more than one million dollars in back taxes the fighter had failed to pay. The rest of the money the former world heavyweight champion earned – at one point in the 1940s, his income reached more than £1.5 million – was spent on high living. He was the prizefighter Ernest Hemingway once described as "the most beautiful fighting machine that I have ever seen", who rose from living with his family in a sharecropper's shack off a dirt road in Alabama to being one of the first black world heavyweight champions in 1937 at the age of twenty-three. He went on to successfully defend his crown six times in six months and reigned unbeaten through twenty-five fights and nearly twelve years. Then, Louis was a symbol of decent living, human courage, and integrity and was thought of as an ambassador of honour and good will for black people – he gave inspiration to a downtrodden people. He was described as a slow spoken, considerate person who carried himself with a simple dignity.

Despite his humble beginnings, the "Brown Bomber" as he was called, was a generous man; twice during World War II he donated his entire purse to charities working with the armed services – he once gave them $47,000. This was something no other boxer had ever done before. He was also noted for being a fighter in an age of bigotry and race discrimination in the United States, where besides fighting his opponents, he had to fight prejudice.

But it was his fight against the tax man that he finally lost: "I guess I owe for ever. I ceased worrying after the first half-million. Now I have an agreement with the tax people in which I pay off what I can in addition to my other yearly taxes. Sure I've spent plenty. But I've also spent it on others. So what? You can't spend it all on yourself . . .," said Louis. He estimated that out of his earnings, the government took about four-fifths and he was left with one-fifth. His fights grossed more than $4.6 million, and Louis received about $800,000, but he saved little of his earnings.

Louis was born on 13 May, 1914, in Alabama, the eighth child of Munn and Lilly Barrow. The family lived in a small shack until Louis's father died and they moved to Detroit, where the future boxer worked in a Ford auto plant and helped his family out by working on an ice-delivery truck after school and delivering groceries. His mother wanted him to study the violin, but Louis was more interested in boxing and used to leave his house with his boxing gloves tucked inside his violin case on his way to his "lessons". One day his violin teacher showed up at his house and his mother asked why he hadn't been attending his lessons. "I want to be a fighter, not a fiddler," said the young Louis. The violin teacher said he would help him become a boxer, and his mother backed him. During the Depression, his family was so poor that his mother had to accept money from a relief centre so they could eat. When Louis received £300 for beating Charlie Massera in 1934, the first thing he did was pay back the money his family had been given – £70. But he

Joe Louis, Heavyweight Champion of the World, before his luck started to run out.

didn't have enough money for the equipment a boxer needs and would re-use his hand bandages again and again, and wore old tennis sneakers instead of fighting shoes.

Though newspaper reporters described Louis the fighter as a born killer with the movements of a cat or a panther, he claimed to actually be clumsy and his mother said he stumbled so much as a baby that she couldn't leave him indoors when she went out to pick cotton because he would knock things over. He said his footwork was a result of the instruction he received from the trio who trained him: John Roxborough, Julian Black, and Jack Blackburn. Louis also said he didn't fight much as a kid, and could only remember getting into one fight as a child. "My mother says I didn't fight, I laughed things off . . . I didn't fight much . . . because I kind of kept more to myself," explained the boxer in his autobiography.

In 1932, Louis fought in his first amateur bout, was knocked down seven times in two rounds, and received a merchandise cheque for $4 for his efforts. He began his professional career on 4 July, 1934 when he knocked out Jack Kracken in Chicago in one round and received $50 for the fight. A year later he fought Primo Carnera in New York, knocking him out in six rounds. He became known for his ferociously crushing left jab and hook. Louis went on to win the heavyweight title on 22 June, 1937 when he knocked out James J. Braddock in eight rounds, becoming the first black heavyweight champion since Jack Johnson. He went on to fight sixty-eight professional fights, losing only three.

His most famous fight was against Max Schmeling, a German fighter whom Hitler touted as the paragon of manhood. Louis, who had lost to Schmeling in 1936 when he suffered his first professional defeat, was determined to win after his adversary made disparaging remarks about Americans and blacks and reportedly said that the Germans were the super race and he was going to prove it. The Brown Bomber was also angry because Schmeling had told a magazine that when he fought Louis the first time, the black fighter had fought dirty when he realized he was going to lose. He knocked Schmeling out with a powerful blow to his back, breaking one of his vertebrae. A loud scream went out and spectators thought it was a female fan of the German fighter, but it was Schmeling screaming out in pain. It took him two minutes, four seconds to dispose of the German – the quickest knockout in a heavyweight title fight at the time. According to Louis, when Schmeling's trainers saw that he was losing, they cut off the short wave radio wires to Berlin because they didn't want the German people to know that a black man "was getting the best of a superman." President Roosevelt told the fighter: "Joe, we need muscles like yours to beat Germany."

Louis joined the US Army as a private in 1942 and fought ninety-six exhibitions during this time. After leaving the Army in 1945, the Brown Bomber defended his title against Bill Conn and knocked him out in the eighth round. The fight earned him the largest purse of his career – $625,916. After defending his title three more times – knocking out Tami Mauriello and Jersey Joe Walcott twice – Louis retired in March 1949.

After his retirement from the sport, life became hard for Louis, who suffered the death of his manager Mike Jacobs and his mother, as well as badgering by the IRS for the money he owed them. Louis went into promoting boxing, but found the money wasn't really there. He decided to make a comeback in 1950, but was beaten by Ezzard Charles in fifteen rounds. His last professional fight was in 1951 when Rocky Marciano knocked him out in the eighth round at New York's Madison Square Garden. After retiring from boxing for good, he tried wrestling for a time, then set up the Joe Louis Food Franchise Corp., a chain of food shops, in 1969.

When his businesses failed, he moved with his third wife, Martha, to Las Vegas where he worked as a casino "greeter" for the Thunderbird Hotel, then later for Caesars Palace. Later that year he collapsed on a street in New York City from what was described as a "physical breakdown". Louis later revealed that the seizure had been caused by cocaine and that he had been hospitalized because of a fear of a plot to destroy him.

Louis died at the age of sixty-six in 1981 of a cardiac arrest. He had been confined to a wheelchair for four years after heart surgery and poor health marked by heart ailments, emotional disorders and strokes. But despite his rather pathetic end, many boxing experts still insist that the Brown Bomber was the best heavyweight fighter of all time.

**• chapter five •**

# EXILED ARISTOCRATS

*A lot of exiled aristocrats started out as the people's champion, only to turn corrupt and defraud the country. They accumulate a lot of wealth by inviting other countries to invest aid in their country and then, instead of putting the money into the country's funds, put it into their own private accounts. Or the "champion" turns out to be a worse dictator than the fallen government.*

## Shah of Iran

The former Shah of Iran held a fete in October 1971 to celebrate the 2,500th anniversary of the founding of the Persian Empire. His wife wore a crown from Van Cleef and Arpels, and the party, given in a special cloth-of-gold tented village for 500 guests, included nine kings, five queens, sixteen presidents and two sultans and various millionaires. The tents were air-conditioned and furnished with Baccarat crystal, Limoges porcelain and Persian carpets and cost more than $100 million. He had Maxims restaurant of Paris send over 150 chefs to carve up the meal, which included over 7,000lbs of meat and 25,000 bottles of wine, and the menu boasted roast peacock stuffed with foie gras along with magnums of Château Lafite-Rothschild.

Little did any of the guests or their host know that within eight years, the Shah would be ousted from his country and living in exile. Still, there were signs of dissent among the people, for those who were looking: the grounds surrounding the party were fenced with barbed wire and troops stood guard armed with submachine guns, and the University of Teheran had been closed to avoid embarrassing protests. A little over one year after he escaped from the country he considered his birthright, Mohammed Pahlavi, the Shah of Iran, would be dead in a Cairo hospital at the age of sixty of lymphatic cancer.

The Shah was a hawkfaced, small grey man who shook hands crushingly and had a regal, pompous air. The man who was also referred to by his people as Shadow of the Almighty and Centre of the Universe, was an absolute monarch who claimed to trace his royal lineage back 2,500 years to the birth of the Persian Empire, and was convinced that he had been chosen by God to save his country. His survival of three assassination attempts by right-and left-wing opponents confirmed to him that he had divine protection. Under his reign, Iran had been transformed from a feudal, isolated nation into a rich, powerful country. Born in a Teheran replete with mud-bricks and moats, he left it a modern city covered with concrete, glass and chrome. He was a tyrant who was also an idealist who tried to modernize his land by instituting economic and social reforms known as the White Revolution. His proposal included ambitious goals such as: a higher literacy rate, equal rights for women, nationalized water resources, land reforms to help break up feudal estates and allow the common man to own land, and profit-sharing for workers. Unfortunately, many of his programmes were either poorly administered or deeply resented, and most of them failed. His dreams were shattered when Islamic fundamentals led by Ayatollah Rubollah Khomeini overthrew his government and took control of the country. In exile, his people branded him the greatest criminal on earth and compared him to Hitler. His successors placed a price on his head to encourage his assassination.

The Shah left Iran with a personal fortune of more than £50 million which he amassed from the country's oil wealth, though others have estimated it was over £10,000 million – more than any other dynasty in the Middle East. While in power he conducted business seated in an historic throne encrusted with 26,733 precious stones in a pink marble palace. He had himself crowned in 1967 on his forty-eighth birthday with egret plumes and 4,000 precious stones in a spectacular desert ceremony attended by an emperor, eight kings, and the US Vice President. The Coronation ceremony cost £8 million. His holdings included about a thousand Iranian villages and enough land to hold Switzerland, with various worldwide interests in more than 207 multi-national corporations invested through the family's Pahlavi Foundation – which they insisted was a charity but was in practice a profitable investment house. Other foundation holdings included banks, hotels, casinos, industrial and mining ventures, and construction and trading companies. The Royal family was also accused of dealing in the drug trade and were said to be exporting Iranian opium and hashish while importing heroine and cocaine. A country known as the "Land of the Thousand Families" because of its fat, aristocratic elite, Iran was extremely disproportionate in its wealth: ten per cent of the people possessed forty per cent of the wealth.

When Mohammed Reza Pahlavi inherited the position of Shah from his father in 1941, he was a painfully shy man who masked his shortcomings with arrogance and came to master the art of politics by ruling Iran with an iron fist. He eventually became so convinced of his own infallibility that he lost touch with his people and wasn't aware of their growing mistrust and that opposition forces comprised of religious fundamentalists were quickly gaining enough power to topple him. The Shah lacked the personal authority, confidence and charisma necessary to rule his nation properly, and was a mere figurehead until the CIA-backed coup brought down Mohammed Mossadegh, who had taken over power during Iran's fleeting democratic rule. Even with the US backing him, the only way the Shah knew of to proceed with his reforms was to have absolute power. He brought in Western technocrats to help modernize his country, but wouldn't trust his own people to help run it. Impatient for progress, he ordered all Iranians to immediately adopt Western dress. He instituted SAVAK, a secret police force which arrested, tortured, and murdered thousands of dissidents and became one of the most notorious networks of its kind in the world. "He was no strongman, but a weak character who wavered between a strict authoritarianism and an overwhelming desire to be liked," said a Western diplomat who was in Iran at the time.

When Iran's economy began to thrive in the 1960s and 1970s after oil revenues started to pour in, the Shah began to have delusions that his country could be a major power and used the money to buy up weapons and build up his army – hospitals and schools were neglected in the rush. The US, meanwhile, contributed to the Shah's megalomania by feeding him arms and industries, as well as a billion dollars in military and economic aid. The Shah began to ignore his advisors and refused to hear any bad news of any sort.

Though he claimed to be descended from the Persian monarchy, the Shah was actually born to a commoner father, Khan, who served as a colonel in the Persian Cossack cavalry and seized power in 1921 in a non-violent coup. In 1925 he was proclaimed Shah after parliament was forced to dissolve the Qajar dynasty, which had ruled Iran for 129 years. Mohammed jar, his first-born son, was named crown prince and was paraded around in uniforms emblazoned in gold. At twelve, he was sent off to boarding school in Switzerland where he began to realize his mystical vision of changing his country for the better. In 1941 his father was forced into exile by the US government for being a Nazi sympathizer and Mohammed jar Pahlavi, twenty-one, succeeded him. The Shah, who had married Princess Fawzia, a sister of King Farouk of Egypt in 1939, immediately announced an end to absolute rule and granted the Cabinet and Iranian Parliament full political power. He was little more than a figurehead for several years. His marriage to the Princess was dissolved in 1948, and three years later he married Soraya Esfandavier, granddaughter of the ruling chiefs of the Bakhtiari clan, a notable beauty whom he later divorced when she failed to provide him with a male heir. In 1959 he married the daughter of an army officer named Farah Diba, who bore him four children.

Shortly after World War II, the Shah passed his first test as a leader when, with the help of the United Nations and US backing, he succeeded in ejecting Soviet forces from the northern region of his country where they had set up a puppet regime. He was forced to escape to Rome briefly in 1953 when right-wing monarchists attempted to depose Mossadegh, but failed when the CIA sponsored a counter-coup. After being restored to his throne, the Shah set about purging the country of protest leaders, including members of the outlawed Communist Tudeh Party. He also expelled Ayatollah Ruhollah Khomeini, a powerful spiritual leader, after a succession of violent riots. The clergyman spent his time in exile plotting the overthrow of the Shah's government and later returned to successfully lead the revolution and oust the Shah.

The Shah was no longer the Aryamehr (Light of the Aryans), nor the Shahanshah (King of Kings), but became a man without a country with a price on his head. After he fled his country in January 1979, he bounced around the world searching for a home, starting with Egypt, then on to Morocco, the Bahamas, and Mexico. Nine months after the coup, the Shah requested entrance to the United States for medical treatment and was granted on humanitarian grounds a visa by the Carter Administration despite warnings that the action would cause political problems with the new Iranian government. The Ayatollah and his followers retaliated at this show of unity with the Shah by seizing the US embassy in Tehran and taking fifty-two of its workers hostage. Carter refused to hand over the Shah in return for the hostages, so that the former leader could be tried for various crimes he allegedly committed while in power, and the hostages were held for more than a year. The Shah was welcomed into Egypt by his old friend Anwar Sadat, after temporarily recovering from his illness, but died in hospital there shortly afterwards. He had always been respected more as a leader by foreign government leaders than by his own people. "He was essentially a weak man who played the role of dictator", said the Shah's former ambassador to the United Nations.

# Ferdinand and Imelda Marcos

Former Filipino President Ferdinand Marcos, who was banished to Hawaii after being ousted from office and allegedly embezzling more than $2 billion from his country, tried even in death to return to the Philippines for burial. He was regarded as one of the most ruthless and corrupt dictators of his time and was overthrown by his own people in 1986

Imelda and President Marcos singing a duet to supporters.

when the wife of his former rival, whom he had ordered
killed, took control of the country. Marcos's wife, Imelda,
a former beauty queen nicknamed the "Iron Butterfly" was
famed for her 3,000 pairs of shoes and million-dollar shopping
sprees, but was abhorred by many Filipinos who considered
her a vain, greedy woman. The couple allegedly pilfered
national treasures and millions of dollars while they ruled
their country. The presidential palace is currently open to
the public as a museum, exhibiting the life of luxury they
led. As First Lady, Imelda Marcos jet-setted around the world
looking for "beautiful things" to buy, including chandeliers
from Vienna and chairs of hand-beaten silver from India.
The palace also contained a private hospital with two kidney
dialysis machines for Marcos, who also had his share of shoes
and boots which were fitted with skilfully built-up heels.
   Ferdinand Marcos died in exile in Honolulu at the age of

seventy-two, after evading attempts by the US and Philippine governments to bring him to justice for embezzling millions of dollars from the Philippine exchequer to invest in New York City real estate. His wife, Imelda went to New York, where they were indicted, to plead her innocence. Marcos was considered an arrogant, rapacious aristocrat who began his ignominious career in politics when, as a young law student he achieved national prominence while defending himself successfully before the Supreme Court for the murder of the chief political opponent of his father, who was a congressman. He was a clever leader who knew how to rule his people. Recognizing their respect for successful individuals and their passive, tolerant nature, he exploited them ruthlessly. Marcos confused his people by frequently changing the method of ruling so that they did not know if he was legitimately wielding power.

Born in 1917, Marcos was brought up a Roman Catholic with a fierce desire to excel in everything he did. His father was a politician and lawyer who taught his son the importance of physical fitness. The young Marcos learned boxing, wrestling, jungle survival, marksmanship, and how to track wild animals. He was a diligent student and a quick learner, winning a scholarship to study law at the University of the Philippines in 1934. After clearing himself on appeal of the murder of his father's political rival, who was killed three days after being elected to the National Assembly, Marcos was sworn in as a member of the Philippines Bar and joined his father's Manila law firm. He became a national hero to the Filipino people after acquitting himself, and enhanced his standing while fighting the Japanese during World War II. Marcos was wounded and taken prisoner in Bataan, and allegedly survived a 100-mile death march as well as starvation, beatings, and malaria. After claiming to have suffered eight days of torture when he refused to betray military secrets, he escaped to become a guerrilla leader. Marcos was awarded two Silver Stars during the war, the second for holding off a force of Japanese single-handedly, and went on to become the most decorated soldier in the Philippines after winning more than twenty medals. His awards were later questioned by US and Filipino officials who were suspicious of his claims, which were later demolished by researchers. After the war he returned to his law practice, which he took over from his father who had been killed by the Japanese. Marcos became known as the country's sharpest trial lawyer, and was subsequently appointed as a technical aide to President Roxas, helping to design an economic development programme. He later helped negotiate with the United States for full veterans' rights for Filipino soldiers who fought during World War II.

Marcos launched his political career in 1949 when he ran for the House of Representatives as a Liberal and was elected as the youngest congressman in Filipino history. Ten years later he was elected to the Senate. In the 1960s, Marcos helped the Liberal party's leader Diosdado Macapagal win the Filipino presidency with the belief that after serving one term he would step down and support Marcos as his successor. When Macapagal announced he would run for another term, an angry Marcos switched to the opposition National party and ran a vicious campaign against his former colleague. Macapagal accused his opponent of being a "murderer, a thief, a swindler, a forger and a threat to the country", but nonetheless Marcos trampled him in the election, winning by a landslide.

With his former beauty queen wife, Imelda, by his side, Marcos pledged to cut government spending and stem the growing tide of Communism which threatened the country. He also strove to repress the crime and corruption which had become widespread. Although little changed for the better in the years he ruled the Philippines, he was elected to a second term with the help of his wife. Born into a wealthy Filipino family, Imelda assisted her husband during his election campaigns by giving speeches and singing duets with him. Marcos's popularity began to diminish when he was accused of polling fraud and 2,000 left-wing demonstrators stormed the presidential palace in protest. Amid frequent protests and an alleged Communist threat, Marcos declared martial law in September 1972 and began arresting his main political opponents as well as journalists, students, and critics, including Benigno Aquino, a popular activist whom he later ordered shot upon his return from exile in a Manila airport. He employed a brutal army to carry out his threats, abolished Congress and rewrote the Constitution, giving himself absolute power. Over the next five years the country continued to be ruled by martial law and more than

70,000 people were arrested. Countless dissidents fled the country and in the 1970s Iran was believed to have more political exiles than any other country. He even introduced a new calendar in 1976, using a base year of 559 BC, the year Cyrus the Great was crowned Shah of Persia.

Meanwhile, Imelda Marcos was busy travelling the world buying up expensive works of art – supposedly for the Manila Metropolitan Museum – then storing them in their Manhattan apartments and their 200 luxury homes and office blocks around the world. The couple also hid millions of dollars in gold they looted from the National Treasury which was reportedly hidden on a ship called the Ang Pangalo, along with many of their treasures. The liner, originally built as a casino, contained a helipad which converted into a disco-theque and was used by the dictator for giving extravagant parties. Control of the national wealth, including coconut and sugar commodities, was given to their friends who invested the money they made in real estate in the US. Marcos gave control of the media to his associates and relatives, who kept the public ignorant of the fact that the country's foreign debt had skyrocketed from $2.2 billion in 1972 to $28 billion in 1986, while unemployment rose to twenty per cent. He ruled the Philippines with an iron fist over the next nine years, with his wife holding high-profile government posts, including Minister of Human Settlements and Governor of Manila. Many believed the former beauty queen was waiting to succeed her ailing husband, who had previously succeeded in deceiving his people into believing that he was not ill.

Under growing international political pressure, Marcos lifted martial law in January 1981 after a visit to the Philippines by Pope John II, though he retained his full presidential powers. He was re-elected five months later for another six-year term under dubious circumstances and seemed to have established an effective method of ruling with support by the US government, which believed Marcos would be useful in fighting off Communism. He was toasted by then Vice President Bush in 1981, who said: "We love your adherence to democratic principles."

Amid rumours that the president's health was failing, a growing Communist rebellion, and outspoken criticism from Roman Catholic Church leaders, Marcos's hold on power in his country began to weaken significantly and in February

1986 he was deposed by Mrs Corazon Aquino, widow of his chief political rival whom he had ordered killed several years before, and her "People Power". The day he fled his country, Marcos gave a television broadcast declaring that he was still in control. Rebel soldiers cut the transmission wires, but the dictator continued rambling on until he was whisked out of the presidential palace and into a waiting American helicopter to be taken to Honolulu – though he pleaded to be taken to his home province in the north of the Philippines instead. Imelda Marcos left behind much of her jewellery and closets full of expensive clothes, hundreds of black brassieres and thousands of shoes. Mrs Aquino, now in charge, began searching for the national treasures and 1,000 tons of gold worth nearly £8 billion that had been allegedly pilfered by the couple. By the time they fled an estimated 60,000 Filipinos had been killed in protests and rebellions.

Marcos, however, was not yet ready to give up and sent money to the Philippines to fund a pro-Marcos movement, refusing to allow the burial of his mother until he could return for her funeral. Her body still lies in a coffin preserved in formaldehyde in the Marcos Museum. In 1987, Marcos attempted to re-claim the leadership of his country by leading an armed rebellion which he was ready to fund. When the information, including tape recorded conversations between the former leader and a Saudi Arabian businessman, was leaked to Congress, President Ronald Reagan ordered that Marcos should be banned from leaving Hawaii with restricted movement. The former leader was indicted by a US grand jury for stealing £64 million from the Philippine Treasury and fraudulently borrowing £103 million from NY banks to purchase real estate.

When Marcos died in 1986, President Aquino refused to allow his body to be buried in his homeland, fearful that it would be a threat to her government's stability. Her government, which seized hundreds of millions of pounds of cash and property the couple left behind, is still attempting to retrieve more than $2 billion they believe the Marcos family acquired through racketeering, fraud and extortion. Imelda Marcos has since returned to the Philippines where she hopes to stand in the 1992 presidential elections there. Her husband will go down in history as one of the great survivors – and cruelest dictators – of this century.

# General Manuel Noriega

In what was considered one of the most expensive manhunts in history – the US invasion of Panama – the American government spirited Panamanian dictator Manuel Noriega away in 1989 to stand trial in Miami for drug trafficking and racketeering. After a lengthy trial the jury convicted General Noriega on eight of the ten charges brought against him. His lawyer, Frank Rubino, described the outcome of the trial as "a new page in American history . . . a victory for US gunboat diplomacy". It was the first trial and conviction of a foreign head of state on American soil. For the former Panamanian strongman, the man they called "Maximum Leader", jail was a far cry from the luxurious lifestyle he led as his country's number one man in the Eighties. "Old Pineapple Face" as he was often referred to because of his acne-scarred skin, lived in the presidential mansions and had French dancing girls shipped in for his pleasure. He was allegedly in bed with his mistress, Vicky Amado, when the US invaded Panama.

Noriega was born on 11 February, 1938 when Panama was virtually under total control of the US. Panama, only thirty-five-years-old at the time, had been carved out of Colombia so that the US government would be assured that a friendly country would control the Panama Canal. Born in a poor barrio in Panama City, Noriega would later become a billionaire and dictator as a result of his ruthlessness and cunning.

After attending a military academy in Peru, he returned to Panama to help the then military dictator Brigadier General Omar Torrijos stop an attempted coup. He quickly rose up the ranks in the military to become the official head of military intelligence, using the position to make powerful connections based on corruption and blackmail. Noriega was considered extremely effective in manipulating individuals and was not adverse to using torture or killing his rivals to get what he wanted. He also began making drug deals during this time. Later, after he became leader of Panama, evidence surfaced that he had forced the resignation of Panamanian President Nicolas Barletta and had conspired to kill opposition leader Hugo Spadafora. He was also accused of allegedly fixing the presidential election. When he began

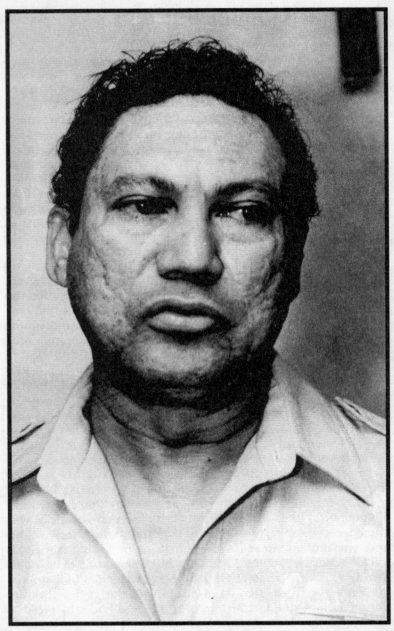

General Noriega, known to his enemies as "Pineapple Face".

to feel the political heat of those who were protesting his leadership in Panama, he arrested hundreds of opponents and allegedly personally shot the leader of a coup attempt against him.

Noriega was not only addicted to power, but to violence, sexual exploitation, power, money and cocaine. He is considered psychologically super-confident, although that may have waned with his recent conviction in Miami. His finances, however, have probably fared better as he is rumoured to hold secret bank accounts all over the world. Tales of Noriega's brutality as a ruler were manifold. A former political rival was allegedly murdered after he announced his intention to reveal details of how Noriega was "a Caribbean prostitute" selling the country to drug barons. The former leader was apparently taking millions of dollars in bribes from his neighbours to turn Panama into a way station for Colombian cocaine lords.

In bringing General Noriega to trial – he was arrested after US forces invaded Panama in 1989 – the US government alleged that he conspired with the Medellin cartel to ship cocaine to the US, protect cartel members from other governments, transport chemicals used in manufacturing cocaine and to operate a cocaine laboratory in the Panamanian jungle. He is accused of taking nearly $4.6 million in bribes from the Medellin cartel. The charges against the former leader were not clear cut, however, since Noriega had worked for the US government when President George Bush was then head of the CIA, and for former President Ronald Reagan when Bush was his vice president. He was paid at least $320,000 by the US government for services rendered, which included helping the US funnel arms and illegal aid to the Nicaraguan Contras in the 1980s. Noriega claims he was duped by CIA contract pilots who used their empty planes to fly cocaine back to the States. But Noriega's involvement with the contras will probably never be known for certain since Judge William Hoeveler blocked any testimony in the trial about arms shipments to Nicaragua. He also ruled that classified records of 1983 meetings between Noriega and then Vice President Bush were irrelevant.

Noriega's stroke of bad luck came when the Reagan administration's covert assistance to the rebels was exposed in November 1986. The general, now no longer useful to the US government, knew too much about their operations and began to be seen as a threat – especially when US policy in Latin America came under intense scrutiny as a result of the Irangate scandal. In February 1988, Noriega was indicted *in absentia* in Florida on drug charges. In April economic sanctions were imposed on Panama, and after a failed coup attempt by Panamanian army officers, American troops were sent in to invade Panama.

President Bush, who ordered the 1989 invasion and abduction of General Noriega, said upon his former ally's conviction: "This is a major victory against the drug lords . . . Justice has been served." Defence attorneys attempted to prove that Noriega was a loyal US ally in the war on drugs through testimony from former US Drug Enforcement Administration chiefs and their aides. On the stand they were forced to read out loud and tried to dismiss the fawning letters they had written the former Panamanian leader thanking him for his unprecedented help and "long-standing support". They tried to prove that they were actually suspicious of Noriega during the time they worked with him.

On his part, Noriega claimed he had been an intermediary between Washington and Cuba and was asked by then Vice President Bush in 1983 to reassure Fidel Castro that the invasion of Grenada posed no threat to his country. DEA chiefs did admit, however, that Noriega's Defence Forces had closed down the Medellin cartel's drug-refining laboratory in Panama, confiscated chemicals used to refine the drugs, and helped catch drug traffickers and money launderers. But the prosecution claims that during this period Noriega also accepted a $500,000 bribe from the cartel to protect money laundering in Panama. One witness, ex-Medellin drug boss Carlos Ledher, testified that at one point the Panamanian strongman was taking in about $1 million a month in payoffs for looking the other way while eighty per cent of all Colombian cocaine shipments were passing through Panama. One drug pilot said he once delivered to Noriega a gift of six dancing girls.

Other witnesses, including former customs officials and cartel members, testified that hundreds of millions of dollars that were deposited in Panamanian banks, delivered in suitcases, or flown in executive jets or cargo flights were allegedly used to pay bribes and buy protection for the cartel and Noriega. The US government has still not estimated exactly how much money Noriega earned by allegedly putting his country at the service of the Medellin cartel, but one witness, a former Panamanian diplomat turned drug smuggler and money launderer, claimed the general was paid $10 million for letting twenty drug flights leave Panama for the US.

Despite the questionable credibility of many of the witnesses against Noriega – many are convicted drug traffickers or are under indictment – and the fact that the jury declared itself deadlocked twice, the twelve jurors still convicted the former leader of eight of the ten counts brought against him. He showed no emotion as the verdicts were read out, and throughout the trial maintained that he was a prisoner of war and wore his Panamanian Defence Forces uniform. Noriega faces up to 120 years in jail upon sentencing. He is also under indictment in Tampa, Florida on a charge of marijuana smuggling and is the defendant in a civil suit brought by the new government of Panama claiming he embezzled money from the Treasury. Noriega has also been mentioned in another civil suit in Panama by the government against the Bank of Credit and Commerce International.

The former Panamanian dictator was found not guilty on charges involving importation and distribution of cocaine secreted aboard a private yacht, but was convicted of racketeering and conspiracy by the jurors, who were chosen for their ignorance on Central America, Panama, and General Noriega. Prosecutors described the trial as just another drug case, and only when the jury was deliberating did the judge publicly concede its historic significance. In effect it was US policy, not just in Panama but throughout Central America over the past fifteen years that was on trial in that courtroom.

Noriega, however, is not the only member of his family to have dealings with the US law recently. On 23 March 1992, his wife Felicidad, who has been loyal to her husband since his arrest and had been faithfully attending the court proceedings, was arrested and charged with stealing buttons worth nearly £200 from designer clothes in a Miami shop. She allegedly stuffed them into a bag of merchandise she had bought, but denies the charges. She was charged with "grand theft" stemming from damage to the clothing, said to be worth more than £700. Mrs Noriega was released on £900 bail.

# Claus von Bulow

After two sensational trials in which his stepchildren gave evidence for the prosecution and Truman Capote for the defence, celebrated aristocrat Claus von Bulow was acquitted of murdering his wife, American heiress Martha "Sunny" Crawford. But in order to avoid any further legal wranglings and to ensure that his daughter, Cosima, would receive the $30 million share of the fortune she had been promised but was denied when she sided with her father, von Bulow agreed to waive all financial rights to his wife's wealth. Three years after the trial, the man whose story was told in the celebrated film "Reversal of Fortune" had sold off the furnishings of two homes he had inherited from his wife. The Sotheby's sale brought the Danish aristocrat £6.5 million, which he now uses to live off in his Kensington flat in London.

Von Bulow, who was born Claus Borberg in 1926 to a Danish father and a German mother with upper class family connections, took his maternal grandfather's name, Bulow, after his parents divorced, and later adopted the more aristocratic "von". He was educated in Switzerland and Denmark, studied law at Trinity College, Cambridge in 1943, and was later called to the bar at Middle Temple and became a member of Lord Hailsham's chambers. Years later, while vacationing in the South of France, the suave bachelor met Princess Martha "Sunny" von Auersperg, the divorced wife of an Austrian prince. At the age of forty, von Bulow married Sunny, daughter and heiress of George Crawford, founder of Columbia Gas and Electric Company in Pittsburgh. Her fortune was worth three-quarters of a billion dollars. The couple moved back to the United States where they lived in the Crawford mansions and penthouse apartments. Von Bulow, however, stopped working and began to feel frustrated by this.

His new wife, Sunny, had been raised by domineering females who constantly reminded her that she was an heiress. She grew up in New York isolated and with few friends. In 1967, Sunny, who had two children, Prince Alexander and Princess Annie Laurie "Ala" by her first husband, gave birth to another daughter, Cosima. By 1978, the marriage had gone stale and Claus was having an affair with a soap opera actress named Alexandra Isles. Sunny stopped going out as much as she used to and became depressed, reportedly turning to drink and relying heavily on drugs. The next year, Sunny lost consciousness at their Rhode Island mansion, Clarendon Court, and Claus called a doctor who performed mouth to mouth resuscitation on the heiress. Sunny recovered, but a suspicious maid looked into a black bag owned by Claus and discovered it full of drugs. She later searched the bag again and, having found insulin inside, notified Annie Laurie and Alexander of the discovery. In November 1980, Sunny was taken to hospital with an aspirin overdose. A month later, during the Christmas season, she collapsed into a coma and high levels of insulin were found in her blood. Soon after, Sunny's children hired a lawyer to investigate the causes of their mother's comas and in July 1981, Claus von Bulow was charged with two counts of assault with intent to murder his wife. He pleaded not guilty when the celebrated trial opened in Rhode Island in February 1982. Annie Laurie and Alexander were convinced that he had tried to murder their mother with the motive of wanting to inherit a fortune when she died, as well as wanting to leave Sunny and live with his mistress.

Millions of Americans were glued to their television sets to watch the trial of the decade that had everything: money, sex, drugs, nobility, servants. It was a chance for the little man to see how the rich lived. Outside the courthouse a cheering squad who called themselves the Clausettes waved "Free Claus" banners. Von Bulow was seen by the media as the ultimate money-seeking poor Eurotrash cold-blooded aristocrat who married Sunny for her money and tried to kill her so that he could keep the money. He was convicted of trying to murder his wife by injecting insulin into her body and was sentenced to thirty years in prison. The Danish aristocrat was granted $1 million bail pending appeal.

On 1 April 1982, von Bulow contacted famed defence lawyer and Harvard law professor Alan Dershowitz and asked him to defend him. The aggressive lawyer, who has been a tenured professor of law at Harvard since he was twenty-eight and is known for defending the poor and oppressed, agreed to take the case on the principle that everyone is entitled to the same degree of defence. He was said not to be able to resist taking the seemingly hopeless case as it was bound to bring him celebrity. Dershowitz, who charged $300 an hour, started work on an appeal and a motion for a new trial with the help of a team of his students he named Mission Impossible, after his favourite TV show.

After the trial, Dershowitz said of his defence: "In the beginning I assumed that von Bulow was probably guilty – most convicted defendants are! Over time I became convinced that von Bulow was probably innocent. Eventually I became nearly certain. This is quite unusual for me: generally I become more convinced of my client's guilt as I get to know them – and their cases – better; and I never become

Claus von Bulow, pictured whilst on trial for allegedly attempting to kill his wife.

certain of their innocence." He said that von Bulow never tried to convince him of his innocence and was open to all avenues of investigation. His research uncovered evidence that the prosecution had not submitted: important interviews with the von Bulow's maid which contained inconsistencies in her testimony, and that the police had not obtained a warrant when they took some pills from von Bulow's black bag. On these points, the Rhode Island judges reversed the guilty decision and von Bulow was granted a second trial in Providence. He was acquitted in June 1985 after Dershowitz's team discovered that medical experts had found that the crystalline encrustations found on the needle used to inject Sunny von Bulow was inconsistent with injection. They also used as evidence sworn testimony from Truman Capote that Sunny had often injected herself with drugs.

Sunny remains to this day in a coma in a New York hospital where her family pays $750,000 a year for her to be massaged, manicured, have her hair styled, and be nursed. She is said to be brain dead. Her children by her first marriage are still convinced that their mother was nearly murdered. To prevent their stepfather from claiming any part of their family's multi-million dollar fortune, they filed an assault, fraud and negligence suit against him. In December 1987, von Bulow agreed to waive financial rights to the Crawford wealth in return for his daughter, Cosima's reinstatement in her grandmother's will which would entitle her to $30 million. Von Bulow is left $14 million, the couple's Fifth Avenue apartment and their Clarendon Court sea-front Rhode Island mansion in Sunny's will.

He has since sold much of the furnishings in these homes through Sotheby's for a total of $11.5 million (£6.5 million). The sale was reportedly the outcome of family bargaining over the fortune and will help pay their immense legal fees. Included in the sale were paintings, porcelain, furniture, and silver from the Clarendon Court home which was used as Grace Kelly's home in the film High Society. Some of the items sold were: a Sir Joshua Reynolds' portrait of Sir Richard Peers Symons Bt, sold for $363,000; a pair of 1822 soup tureens made by Paul Storr, with mermen and mermaids riding on dolphins as handles, sold for $924,000; a Longton Hall tureen dating back to the 1750s and in the shape of a melon, sold for $17,600.

After the trial, Alan Dershowitz wrote a best-selling book

based on the story and his experiences called Reversal of
Fortune, which was later turned into a widely publicized and
critically acclaimed film of the same title, starring Jeremy Irons
as von Bulow and Glenn Close as his wife. "Jeremy Irons is a
better Claus von Bulow than Claus von Bulow," Dershowitz
was later quoted as saying. Acclaimed actor Ron Silver
portrayed Dershowitz, the slightly rumpled, mustachioed,
rebellious lawyer whom the film focused on. Though he
claims that von Bulow urged him to write the book and was
supportive of the film, desperate to set the record straight, the
Danish aristocrat reportedly told a London newspaper that it
was "inhuman and brutal" for the film to be made at all and
is said not to be happy with the movie because it does not
advertise his innocence. Dershowitz disputes this and says
von Bulow's words were taken out of context, and that he
actually thanks him for freeing him from a jail sentence. Von
Bulow reportedly told a friend after the film was released: "I
emerge as innocent and framed and as a shit. And I'm not
that kind of shit."

Dershowitz, who says he uses celebrities to get attention and teach America about civil rights, has since been
retained to defend boxing champion Mike Tyson and hotel
queen Leona Helmsley on appeal. Mrs Helmsley has asked
Dershowitz to write a book about her, too, he said.

Von Bulow, who has been cut-off from the Crawford family
fortune, now lives a quiet bachelor's life in London near his
daughter Cosima. He has agreed with his step-children not
to speak to the Press or write his memoirs.